The Great Magic Ink-Quest

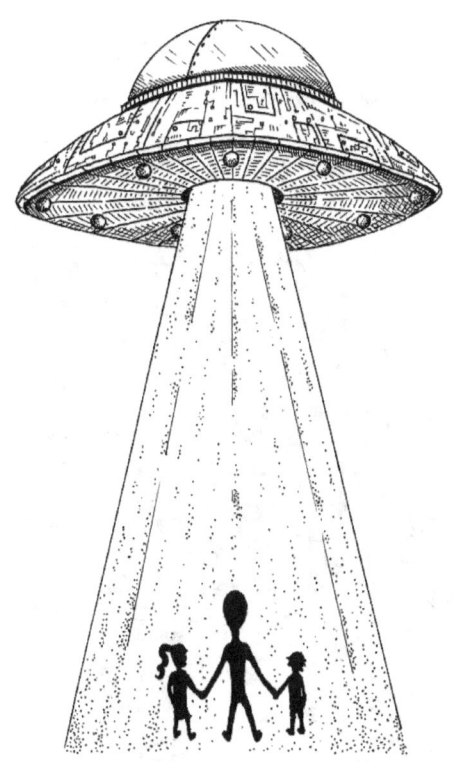

A collection of doodles by

Kevin McKie

ISBN 978-1519419446

Email: kevmckie@msn.com

Instagram – kevsdoodlemagic

YouTube – Kevs Doodle Magic

Facebook.com/doodlemagic

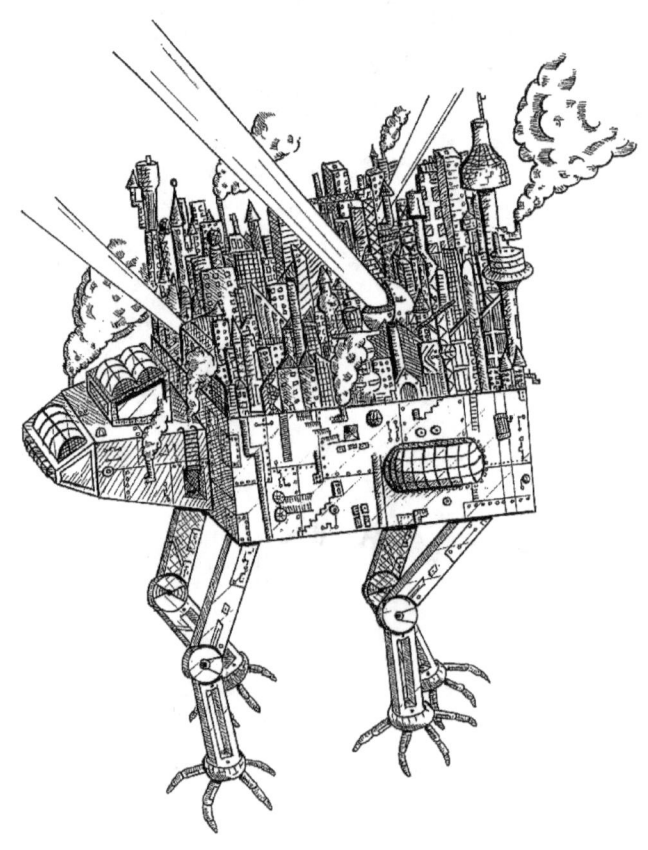

Welcome to the great magic ink-quest

Here lies, within the crisp white pages, a collection of short, medium and large sized doodles plus a few commissioned pieces from my collection of sketches over the past year.

I began drawing in the December of 2014 as a hobby. It was something to pass the time, to keep my idle hands busy and my wondering mind from running away with my sanity.

After receiving a humbling amount of positivity online, I decided to take my work a little more seriously. I now enjoy creating time lapse drawing videos for my YouTube channel under the sobriquet "Kev's Doodle Magic".

My weapon of choice is a fine line marker pen. The contrast of black ink on white paper excites me and brings out my most creative side. I will, however, draw on anything, not just on paper.

Sometimes a 30 minute doodle that I do on my hand can become the best thing that I've drawn in days.

I hope that my psychedelic space patterns will inspire you to pick up a pen and begin to scribble, hatch and dot a cacophonic explosion of ink onto whatever surface you have available. Be it paper, your hand, a coffee cup or the remains from a U.F.O crash site.

Just remember to have fun with your art. Never get lost in comparing your work to other artist's creations. There are too many great artists and their art is purely subjective. Somebody somewhere will love your work. I have witnessed art that looked as though It had been created by a two year old, yet was valued at over a million pounds. I have also witnessed artwork that I could never replicate and was worth no more than 10 Instagram likes. Don't be too critical of others creations

I hope you enjoy what follows…

Table of Contents

Table of Contents

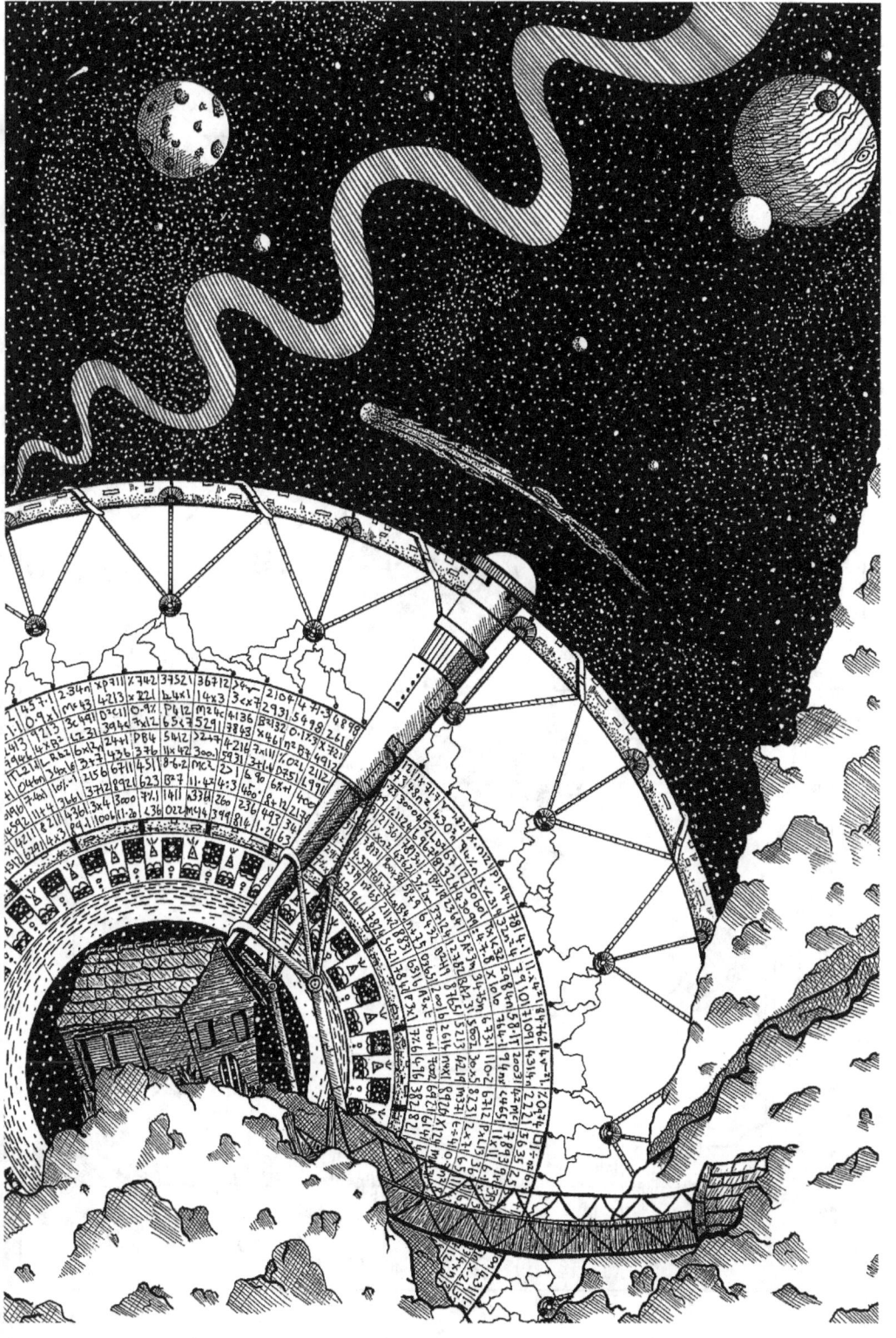

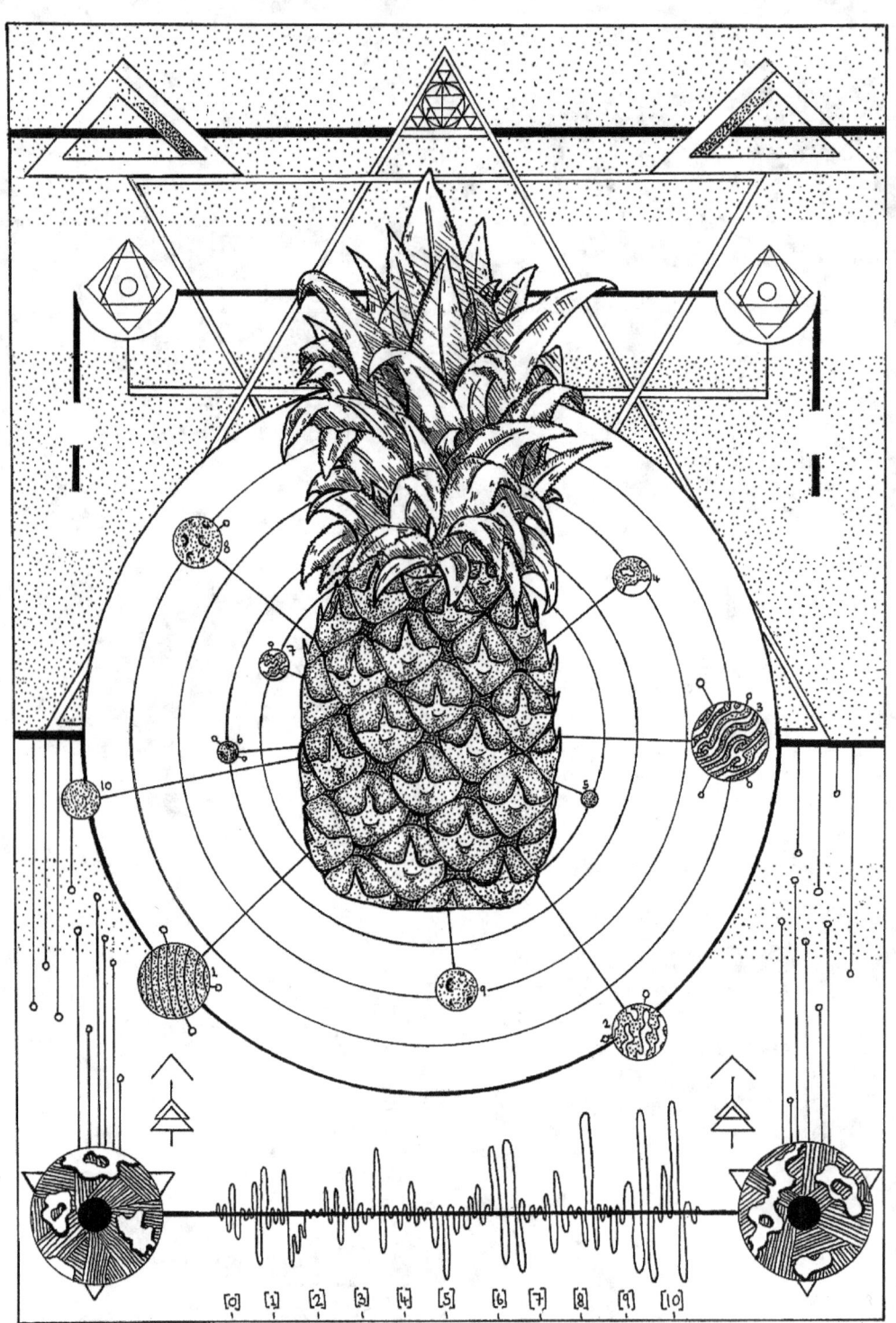

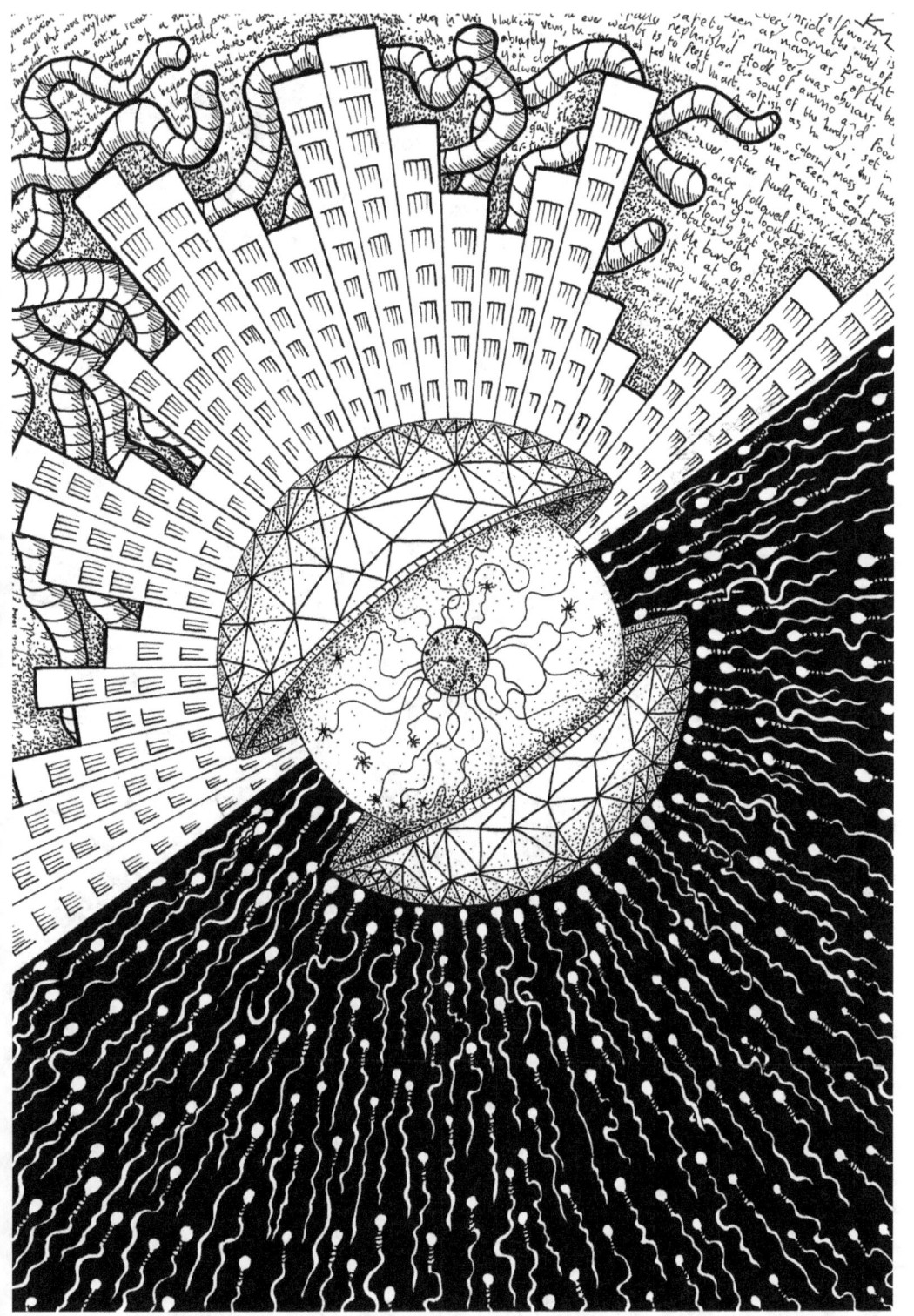

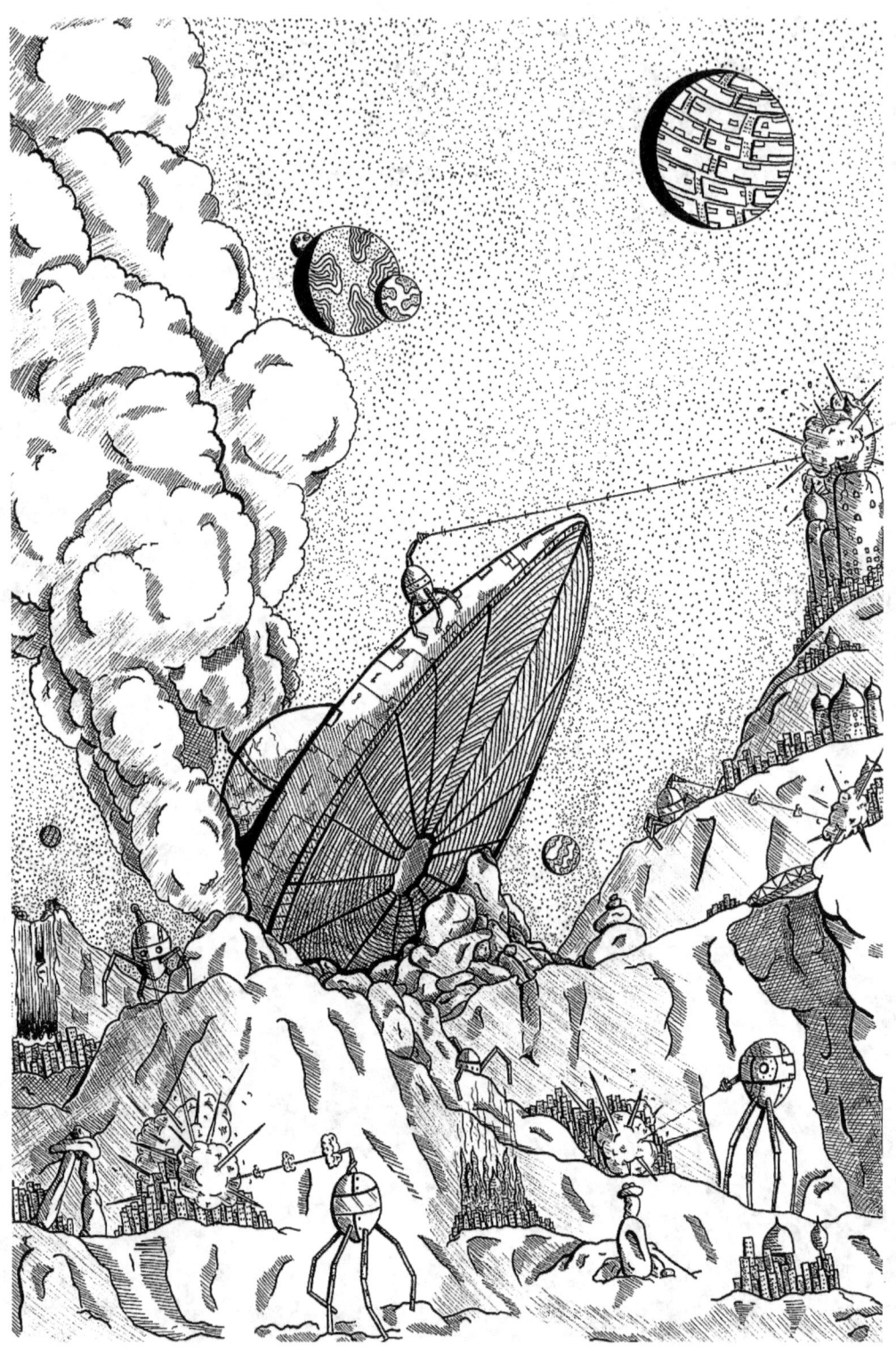

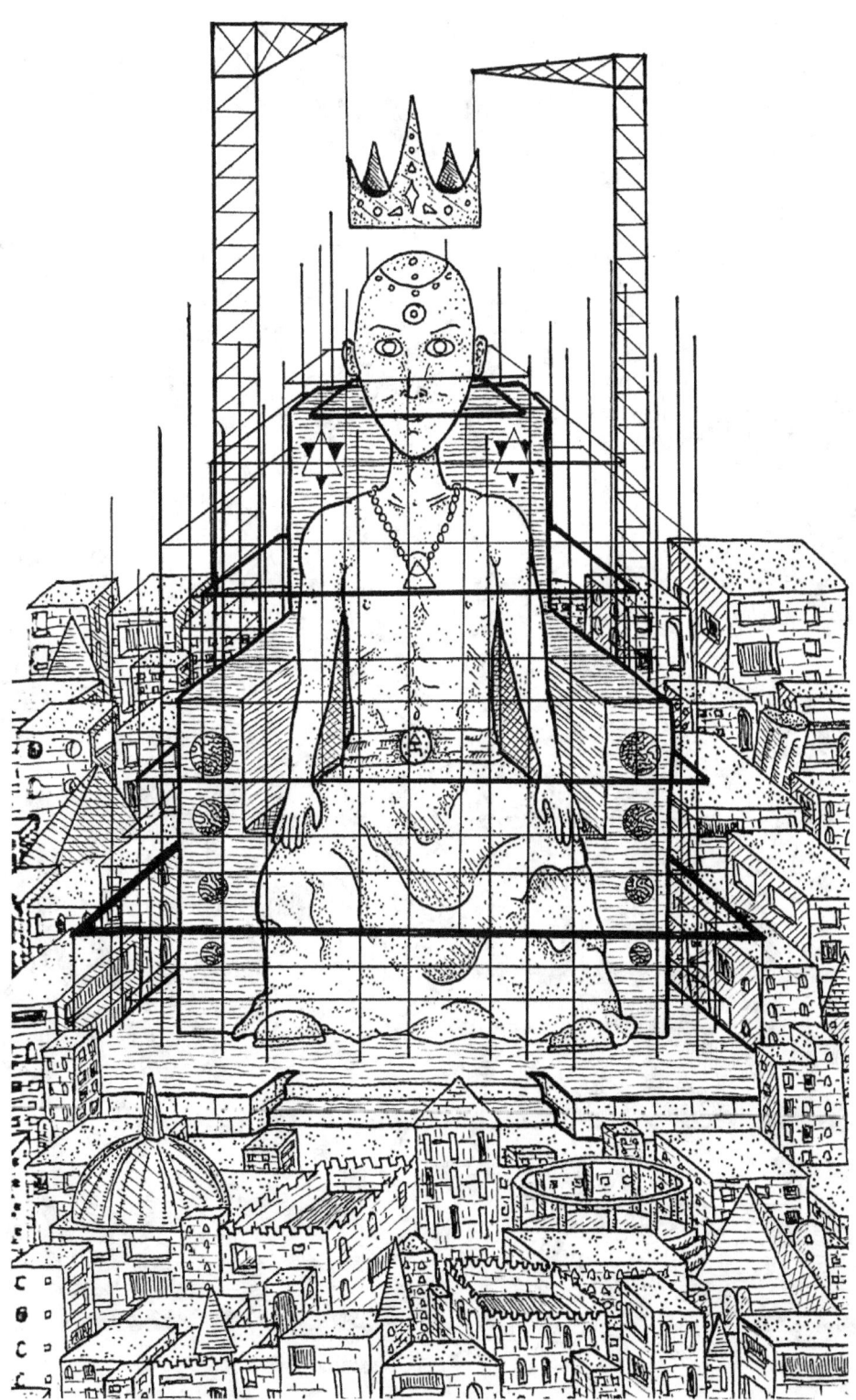

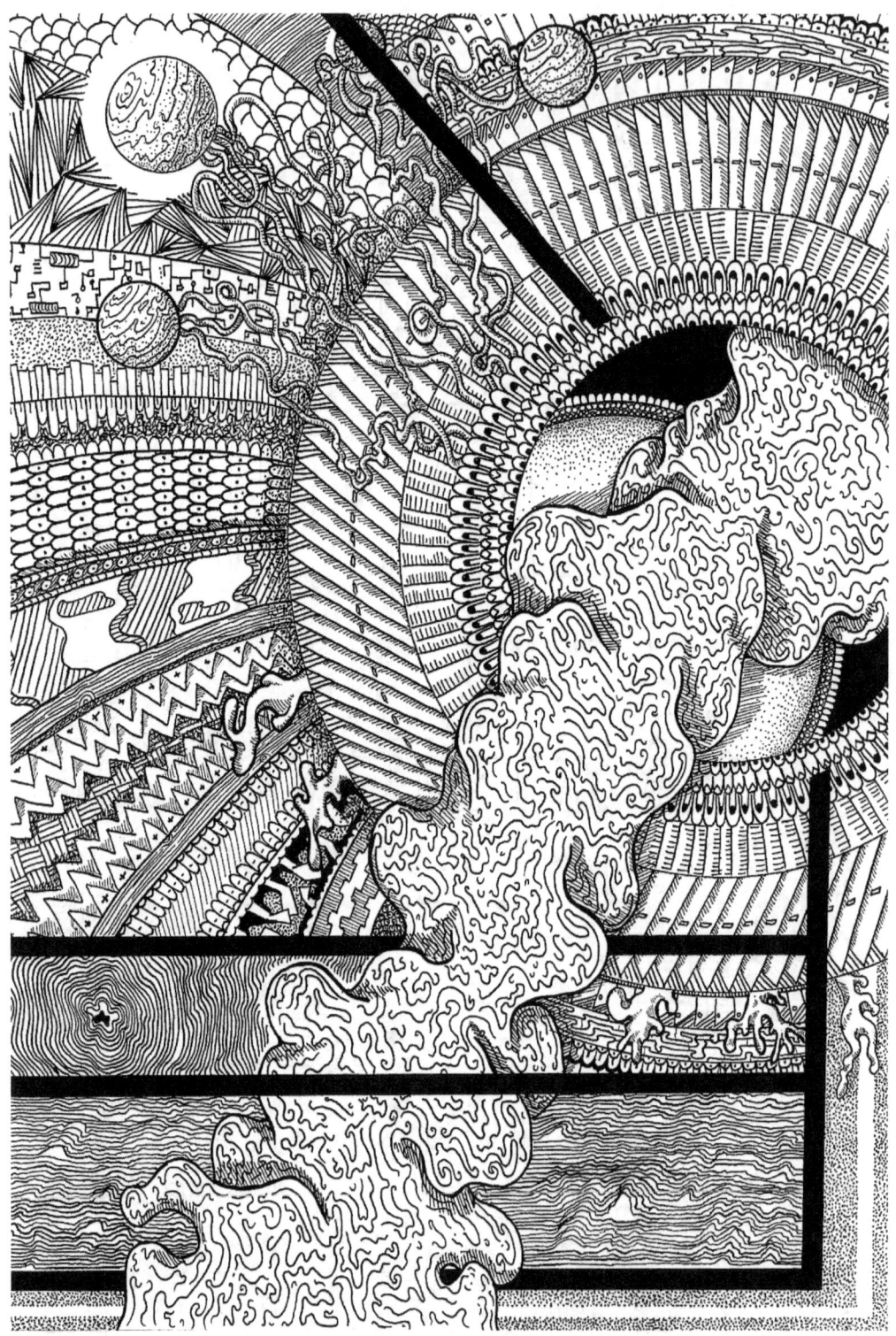

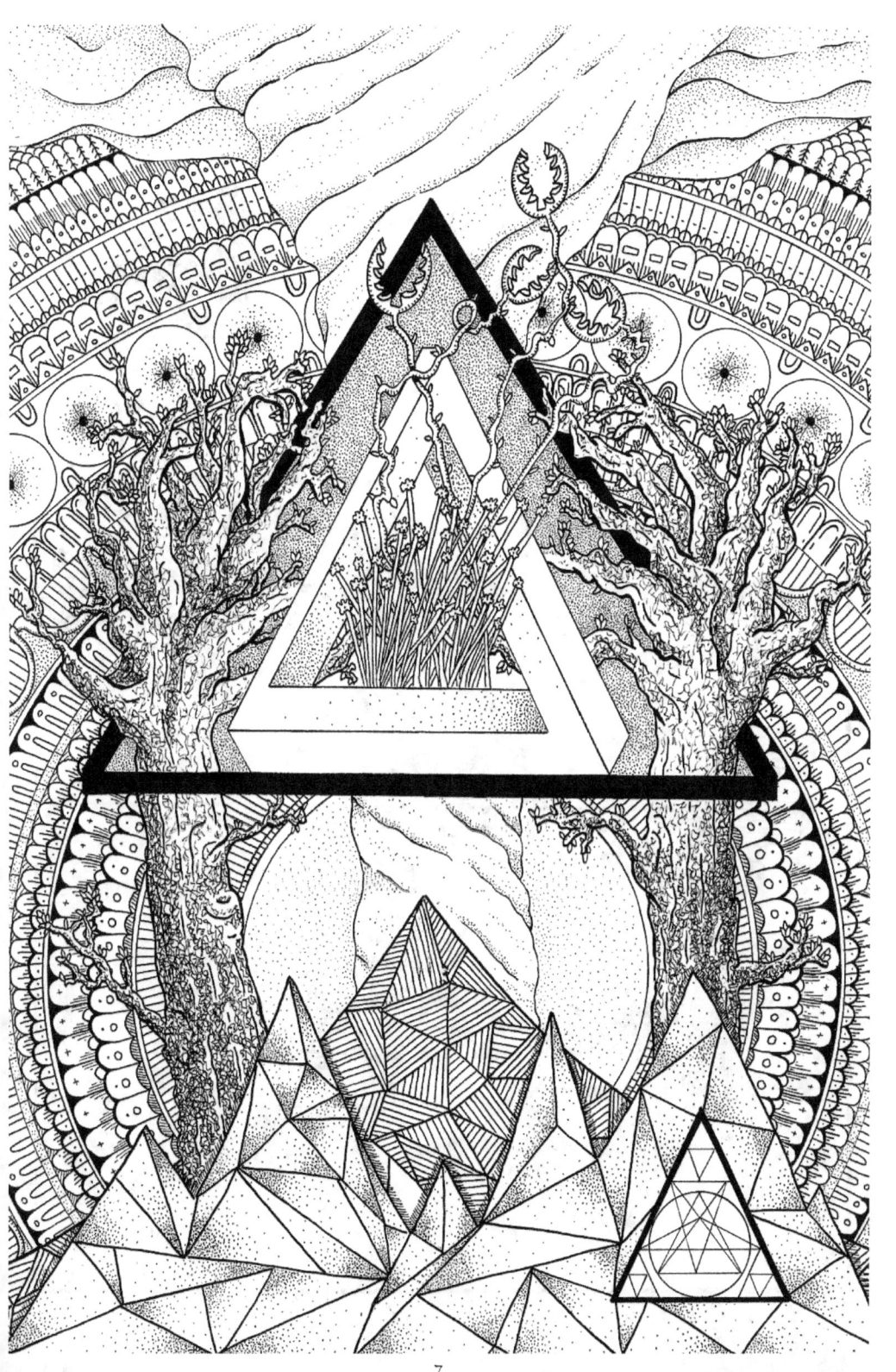

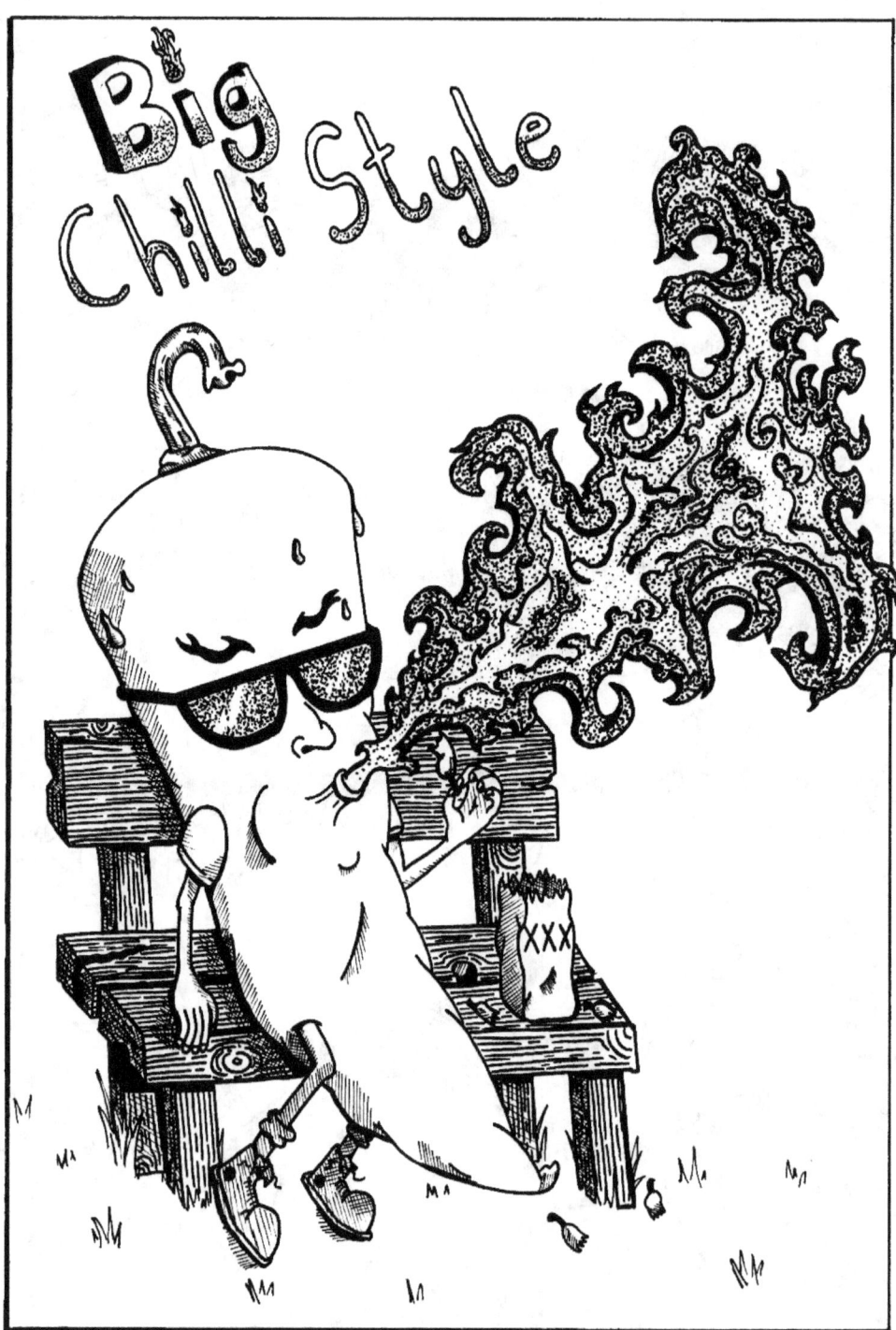

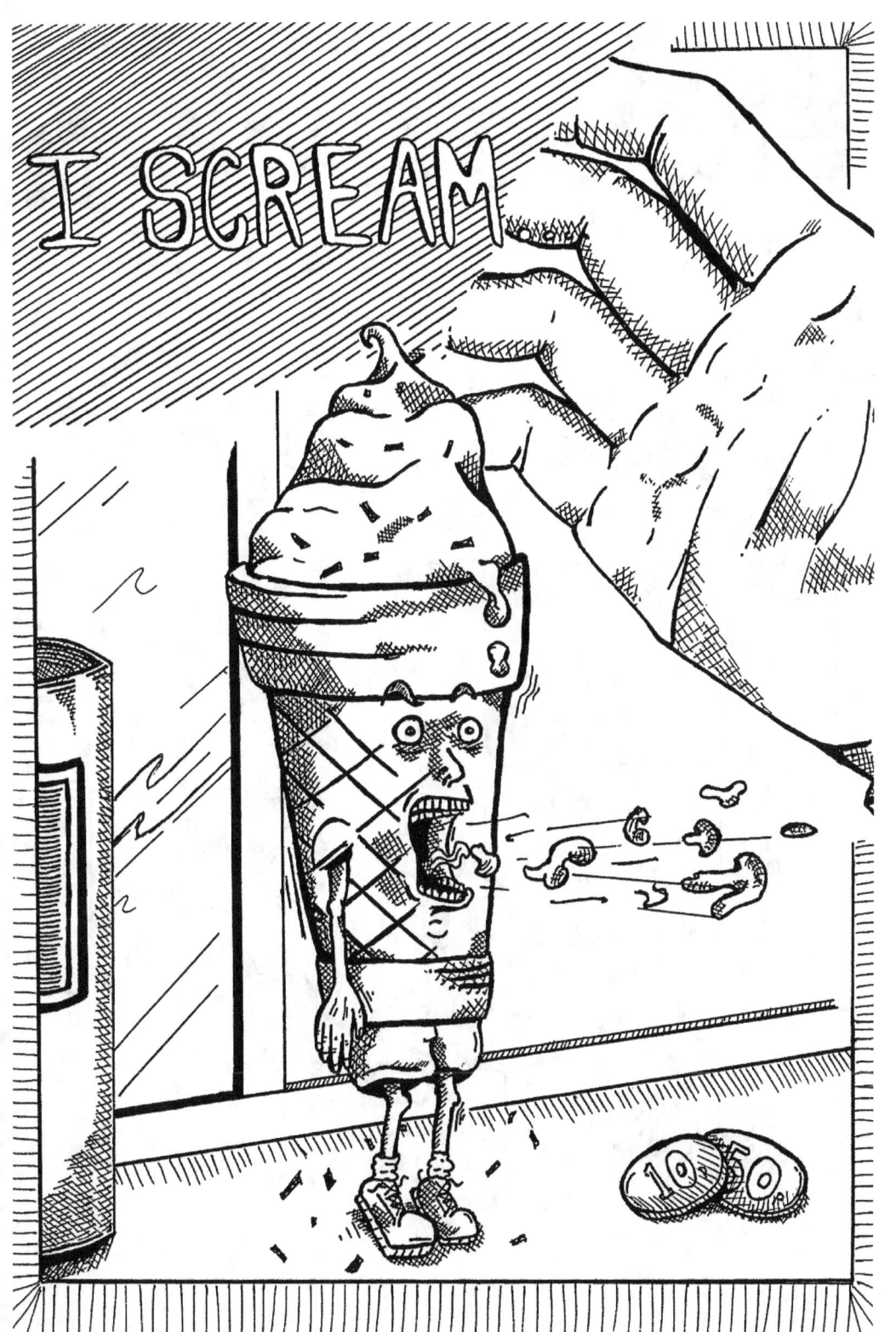

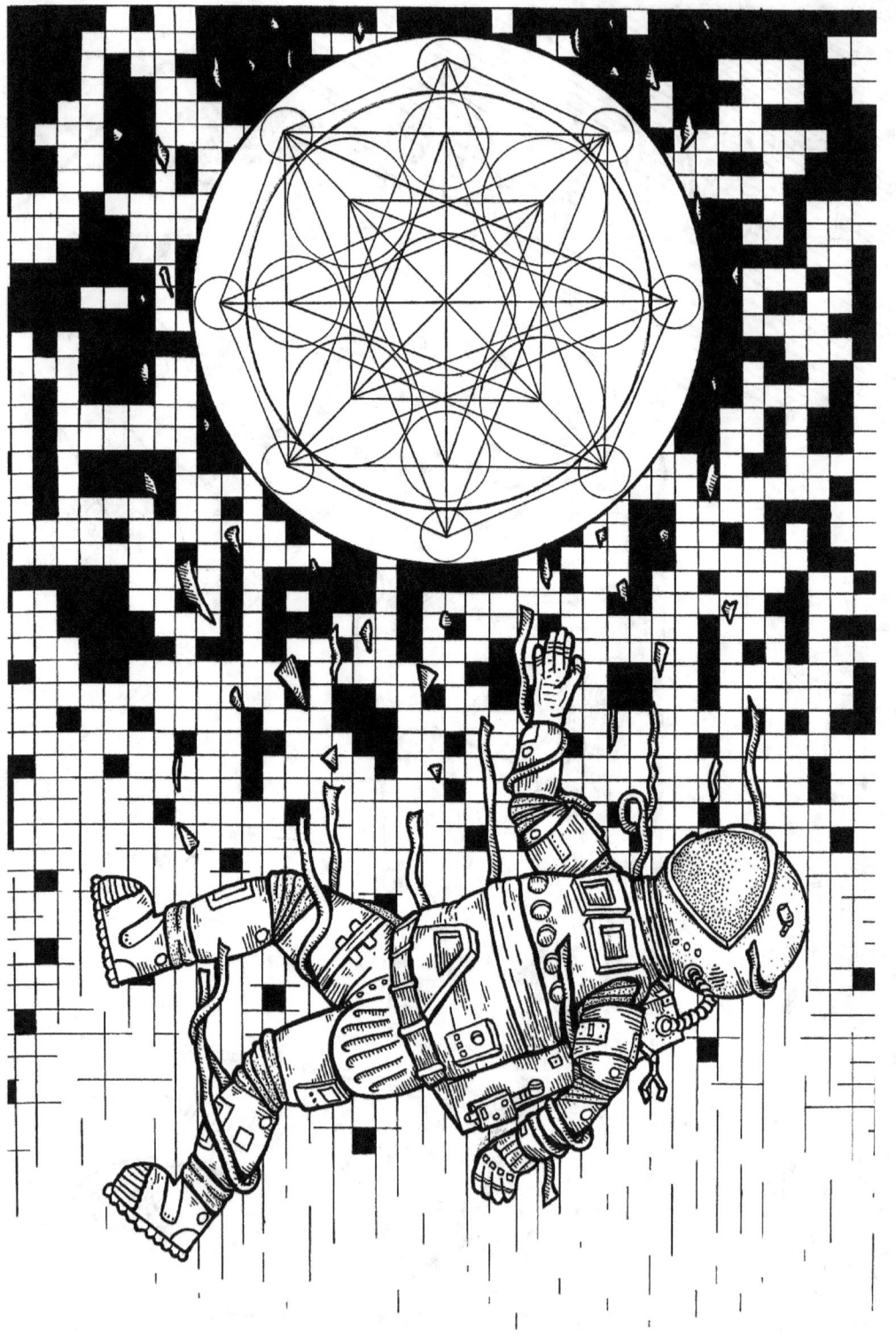

KMcf

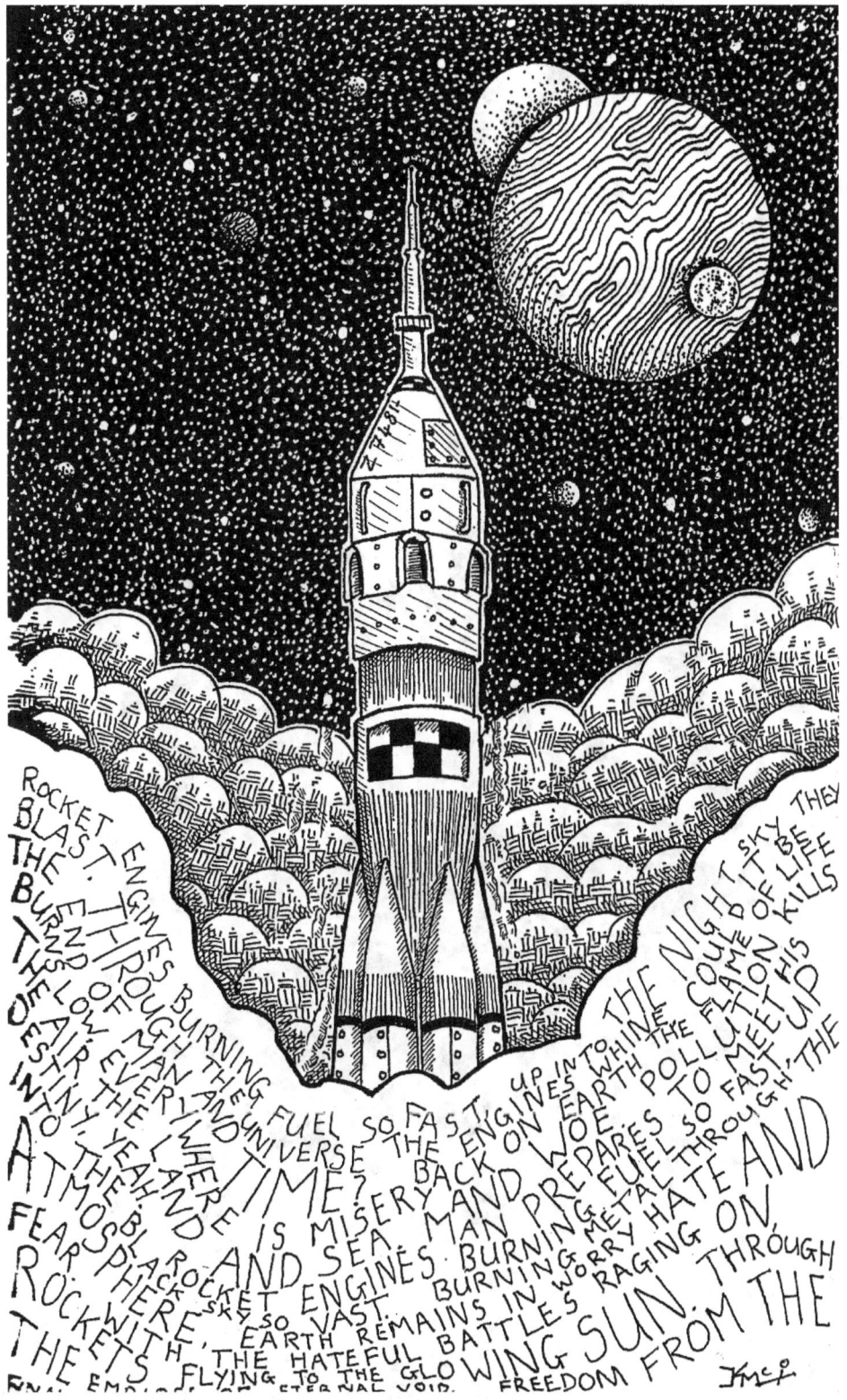

ROCKET ENGINES BURNING FUEL SO FAST, UP INTO THE NIGHT SKY THEY BLAST. THROUGH THE ENGINES WHINE THE FLAME OF LIFE COULD IT BE THE END OF MAN AND THE UNIVERSE THE BACK ON EARTH POLLUTION KILLS THE BURNS LOW, EVERYWHERE IS TIME? IS MISERY AND WOE. MAN PREPARES TO MEET HIS THE AIR, THE LAND AND SEA MAN BURNING METAL THROUGH THE DESTINY, YEAH. THE BLACK ENGINES BURNING FUEL SO FAST UP INTO THE ROCKET SKY SO VAST BURNING FUEL SO FAST, AND ATMOSPHERE, EARTH REMAINS IN WORRY HATE AND FEAR. ROCKET WITH THE HATEFUL BATTLES RAGING ON. THROUGH THE JETS FLYING TO THE GLOWING SUN. FREEDOM FROM THE FINAL END OF THE ETERNAL VOID.

JMCi

11

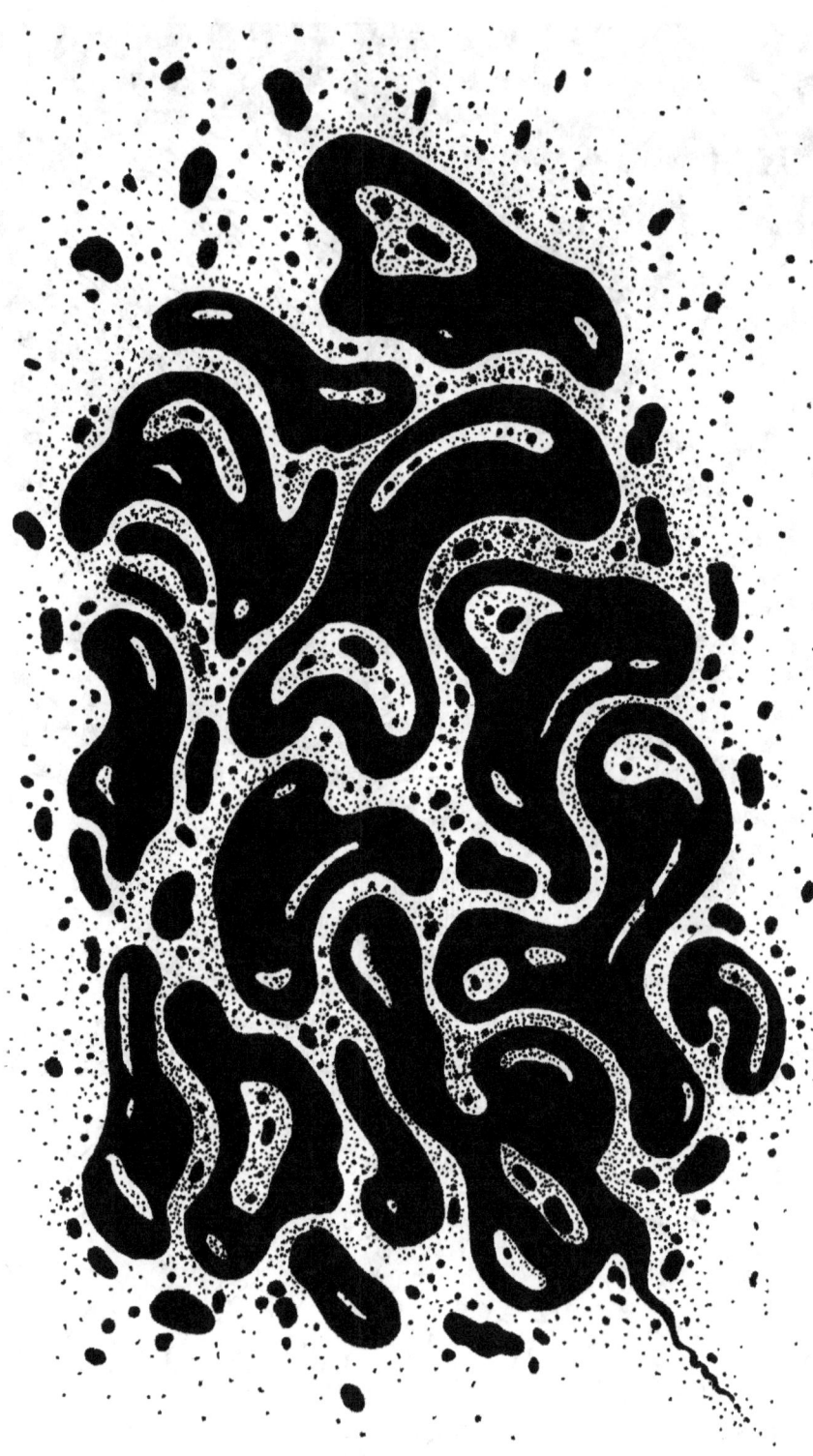

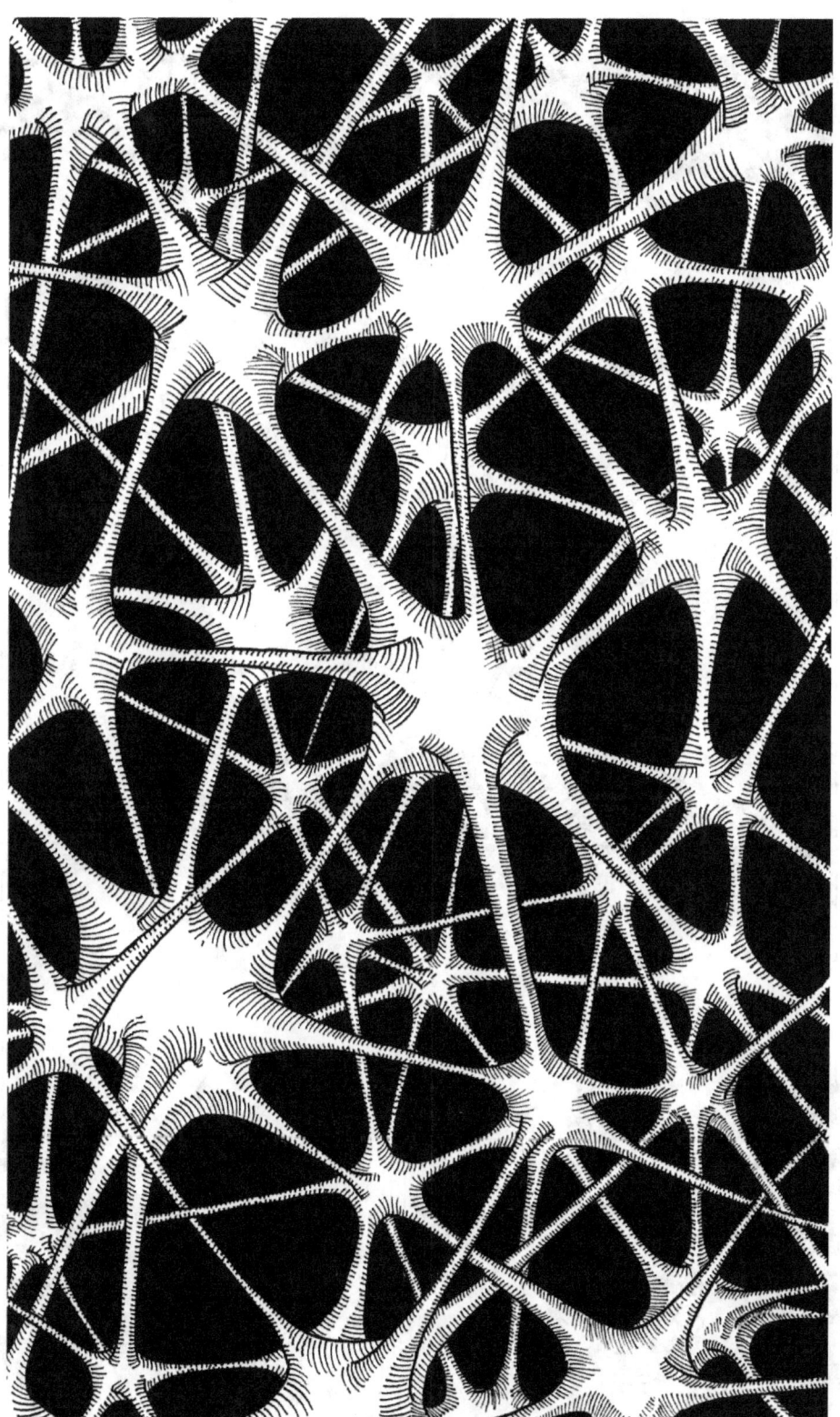

13

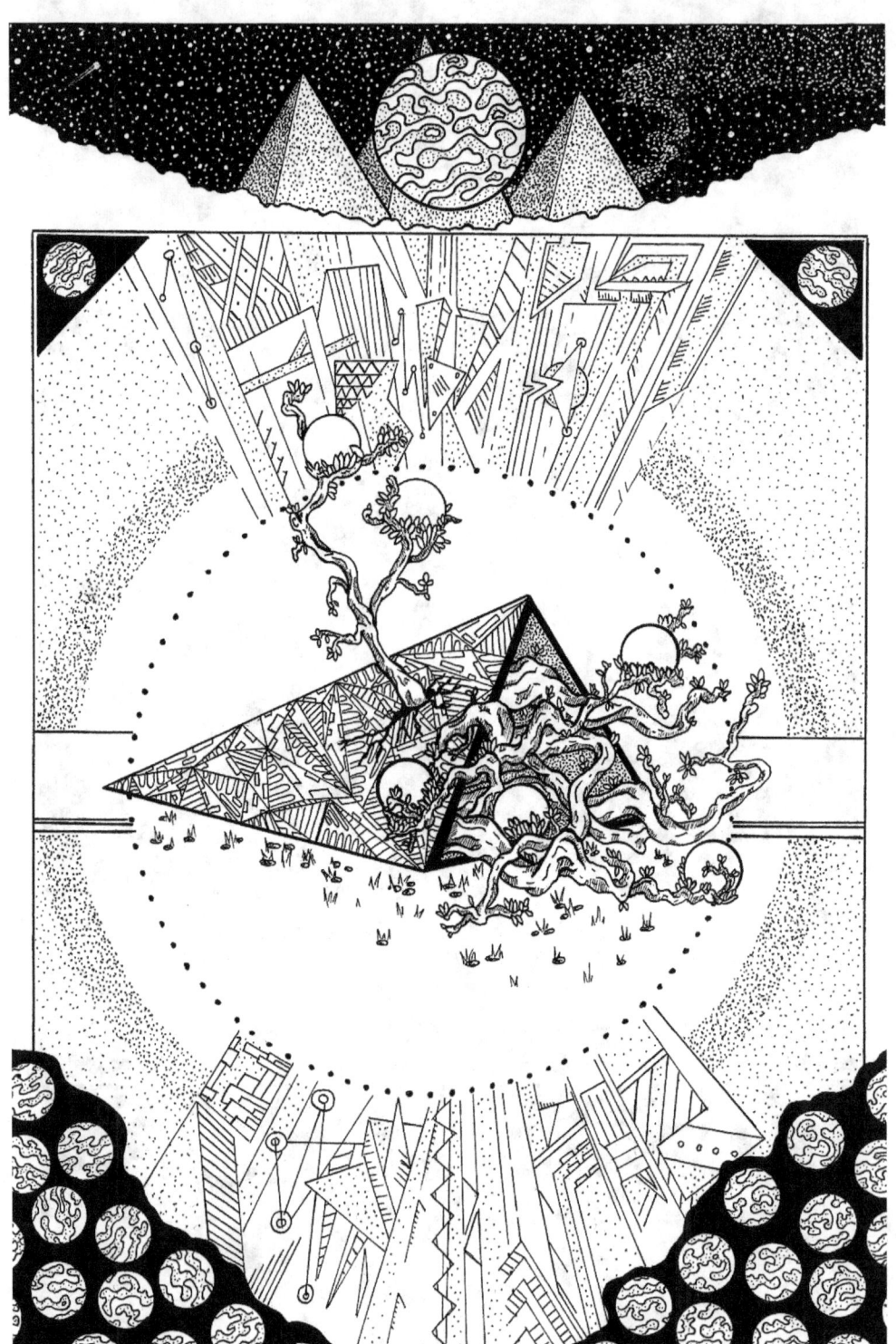

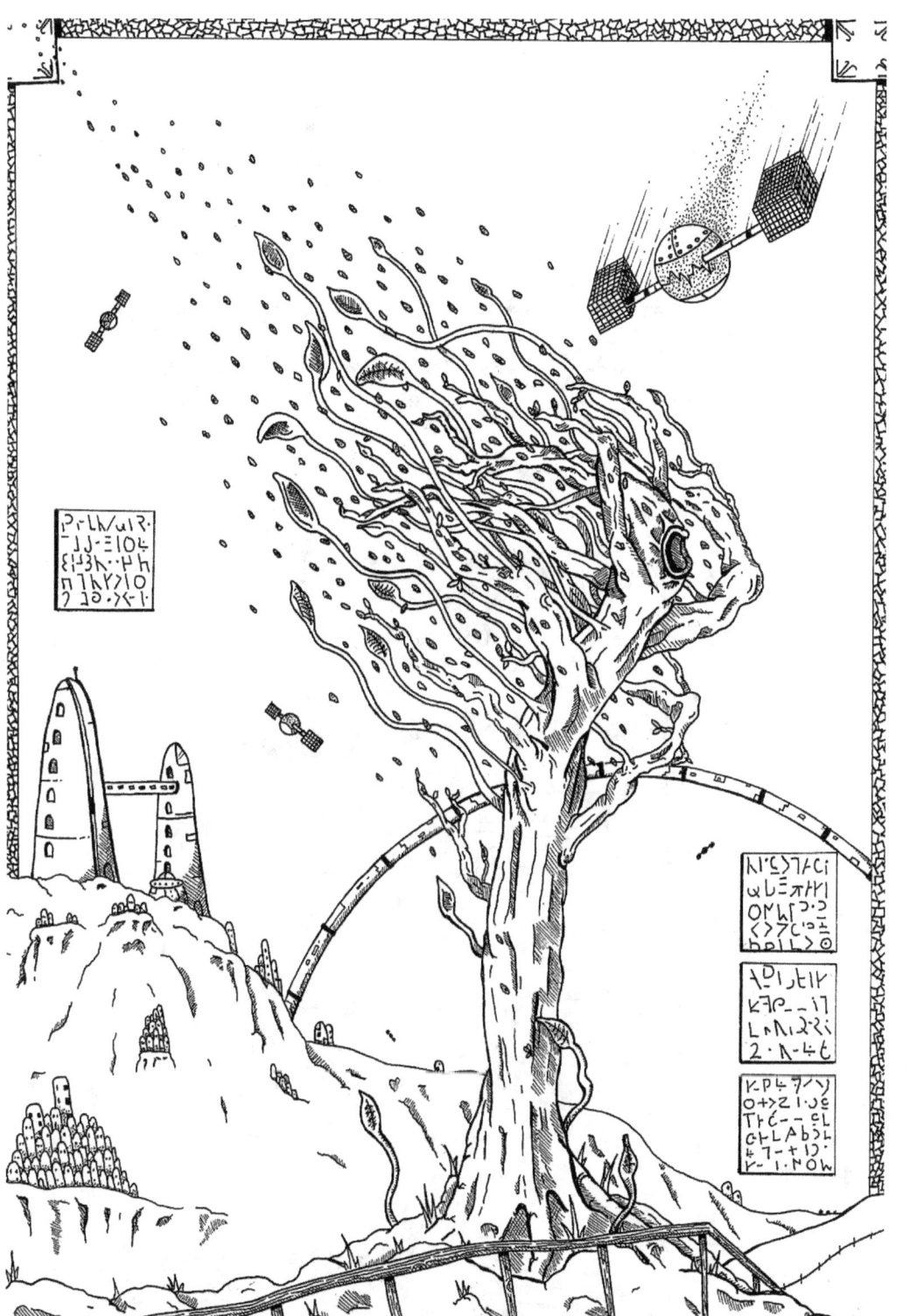

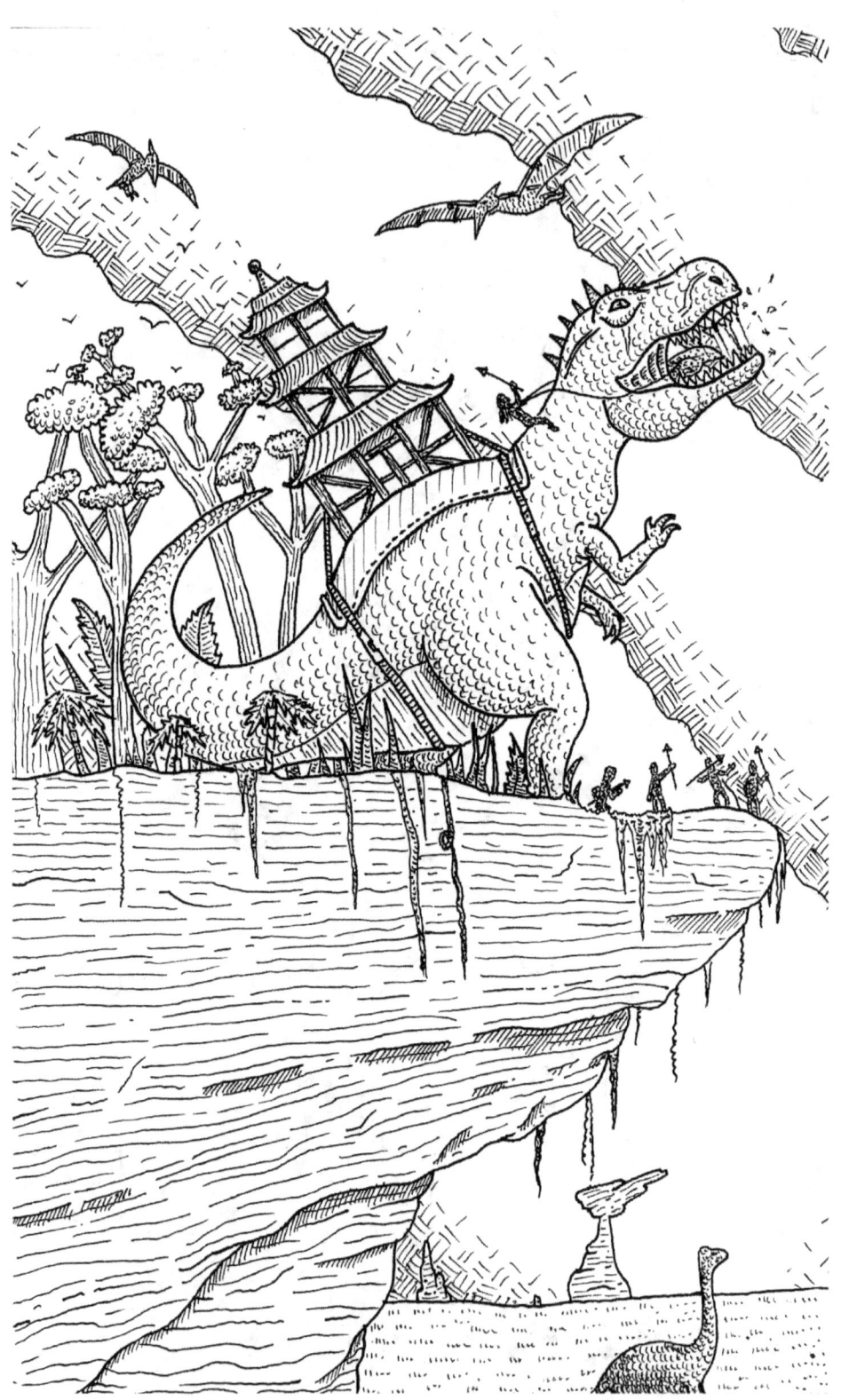

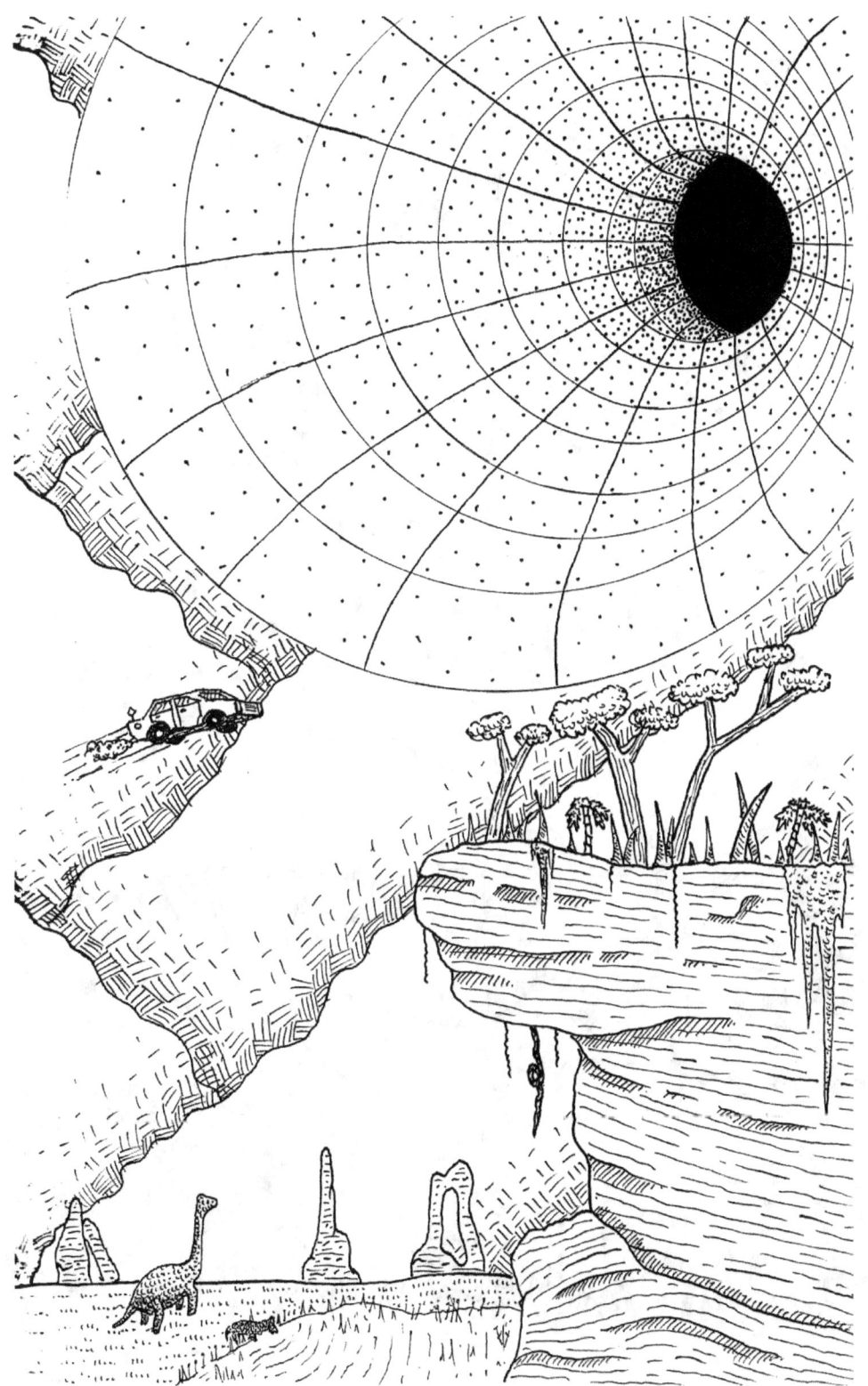

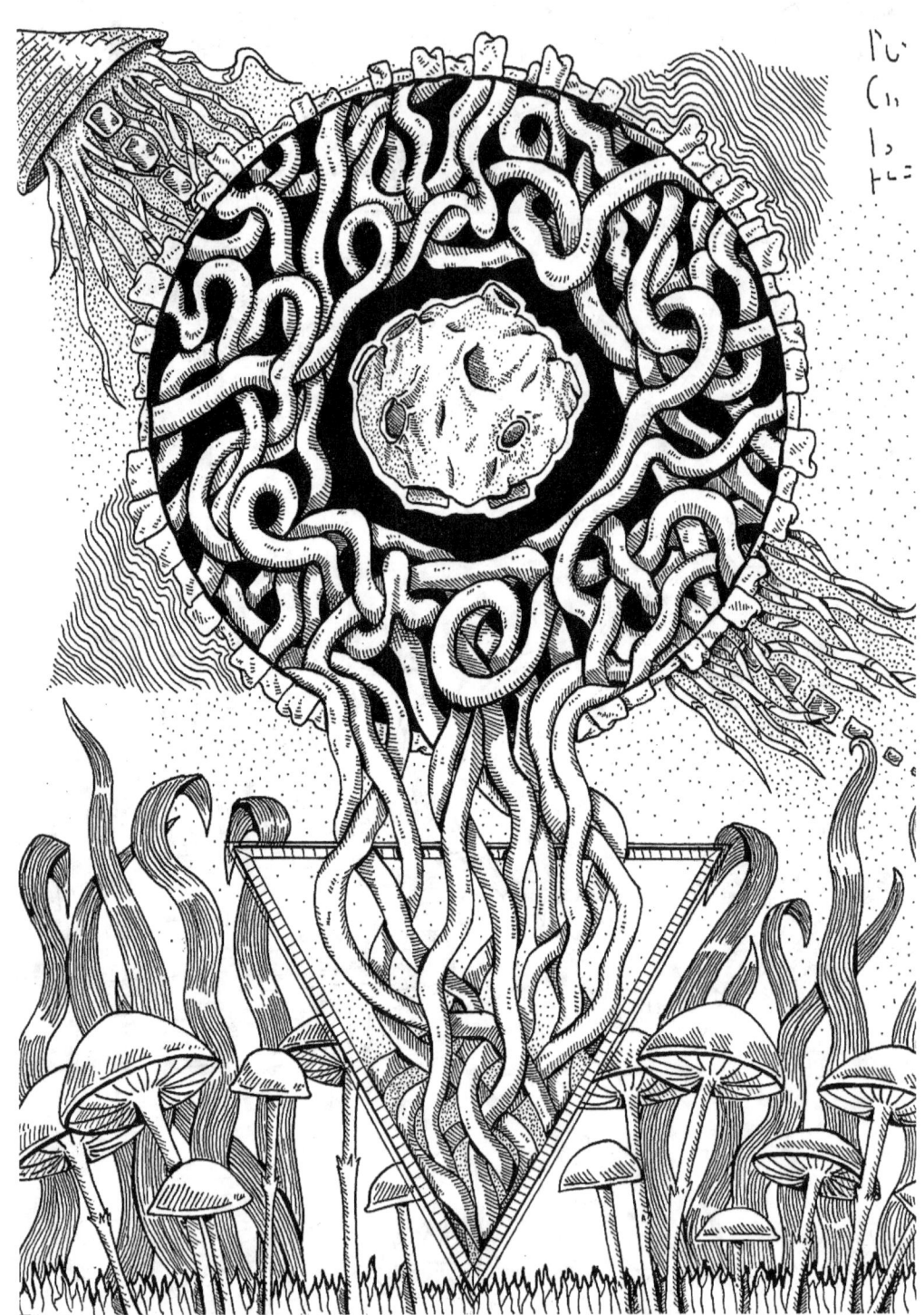

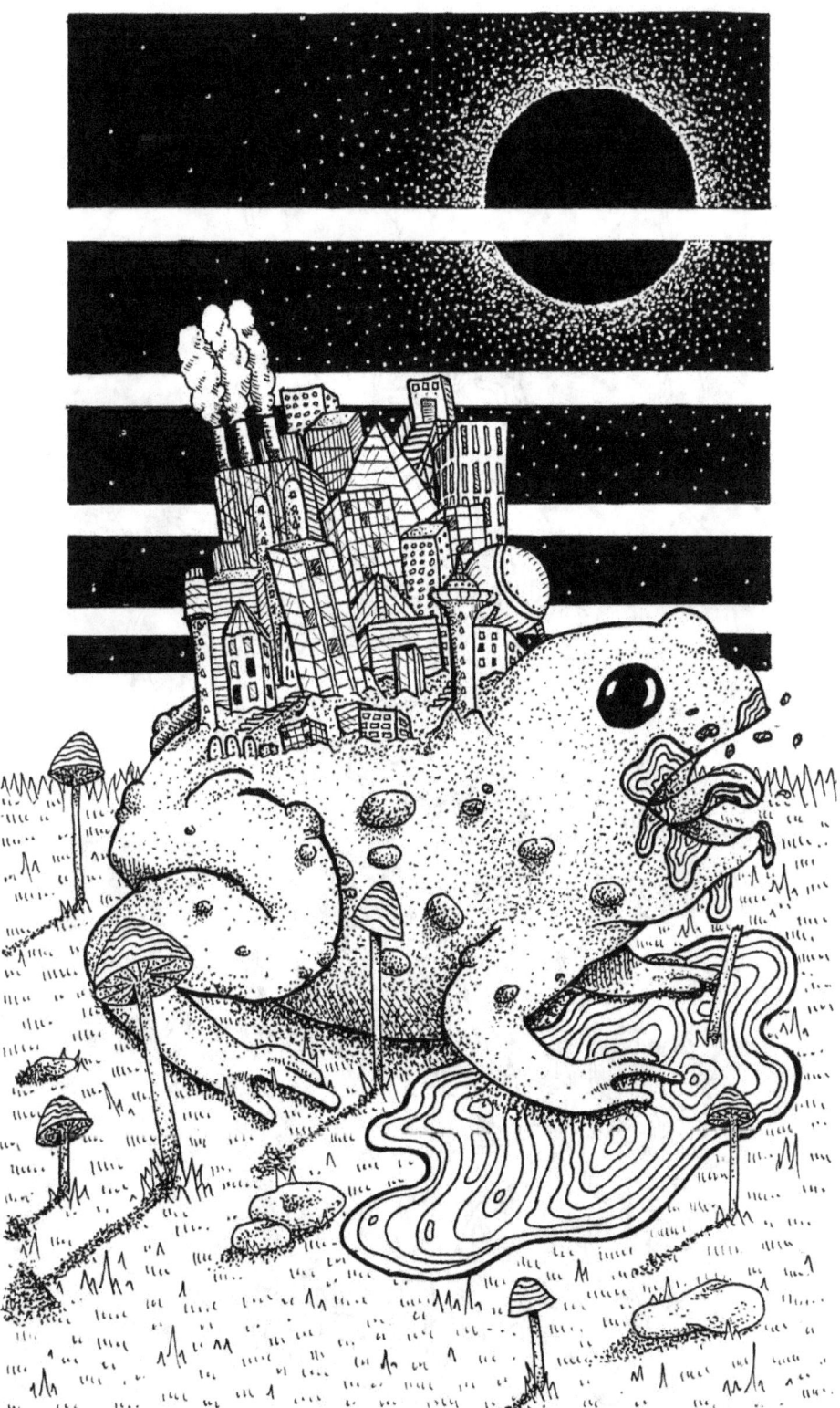

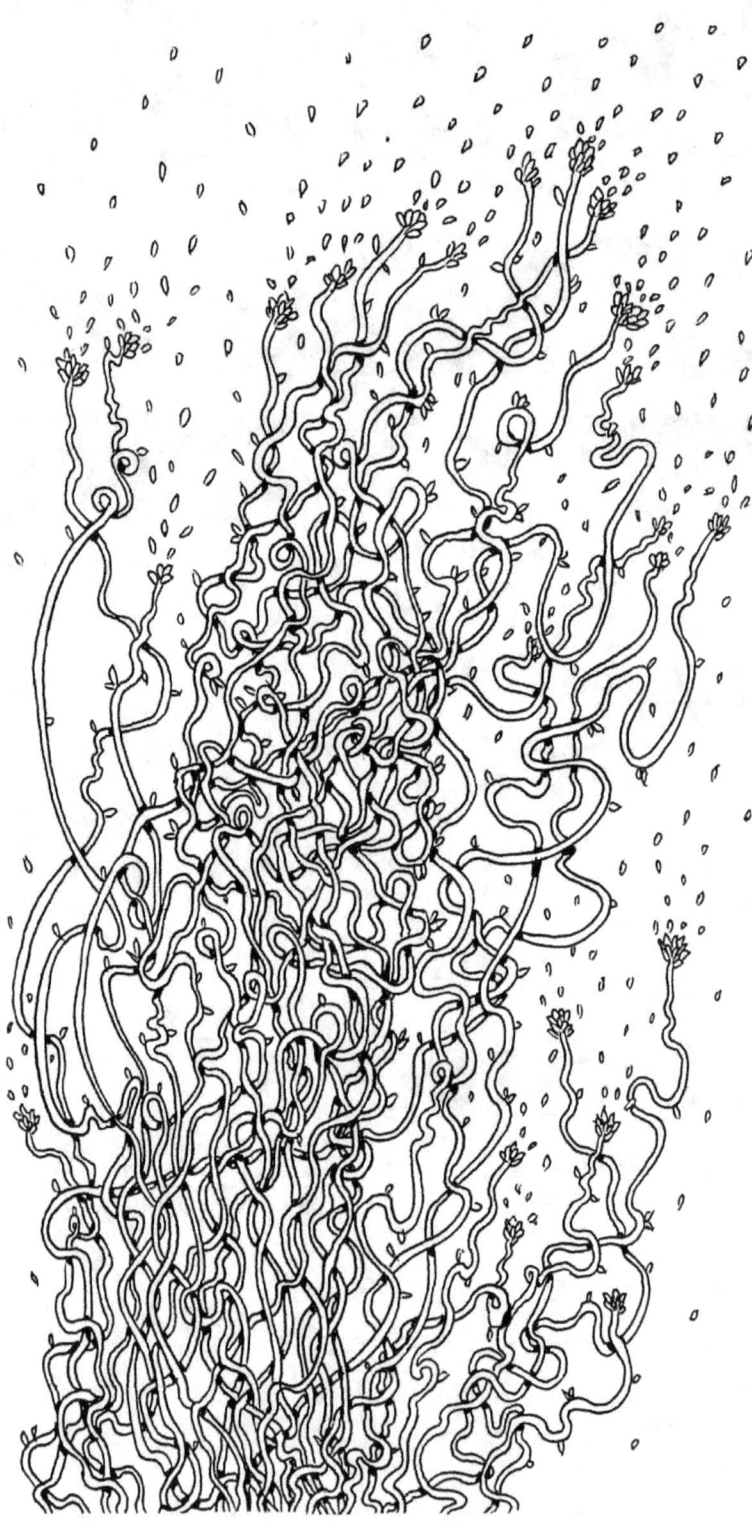

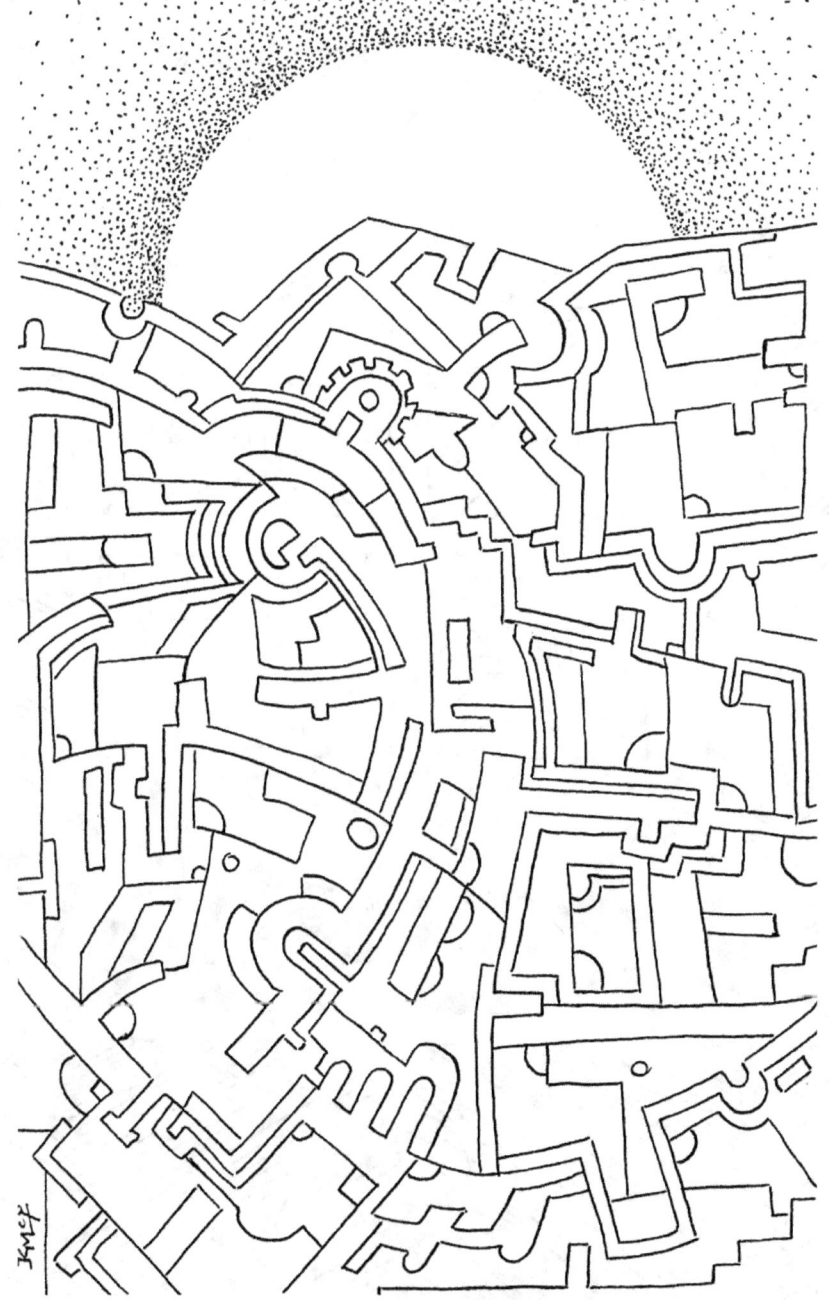

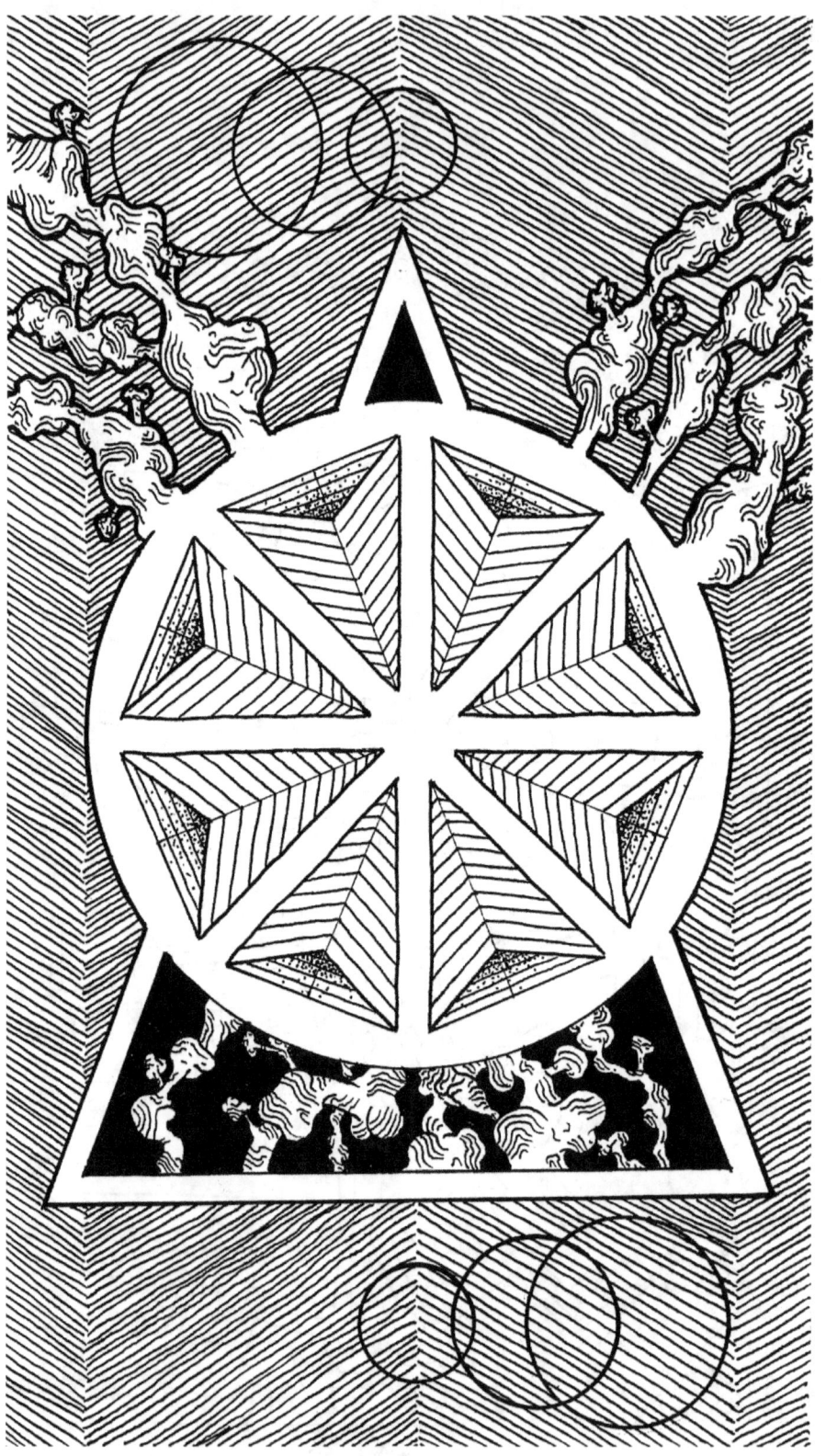

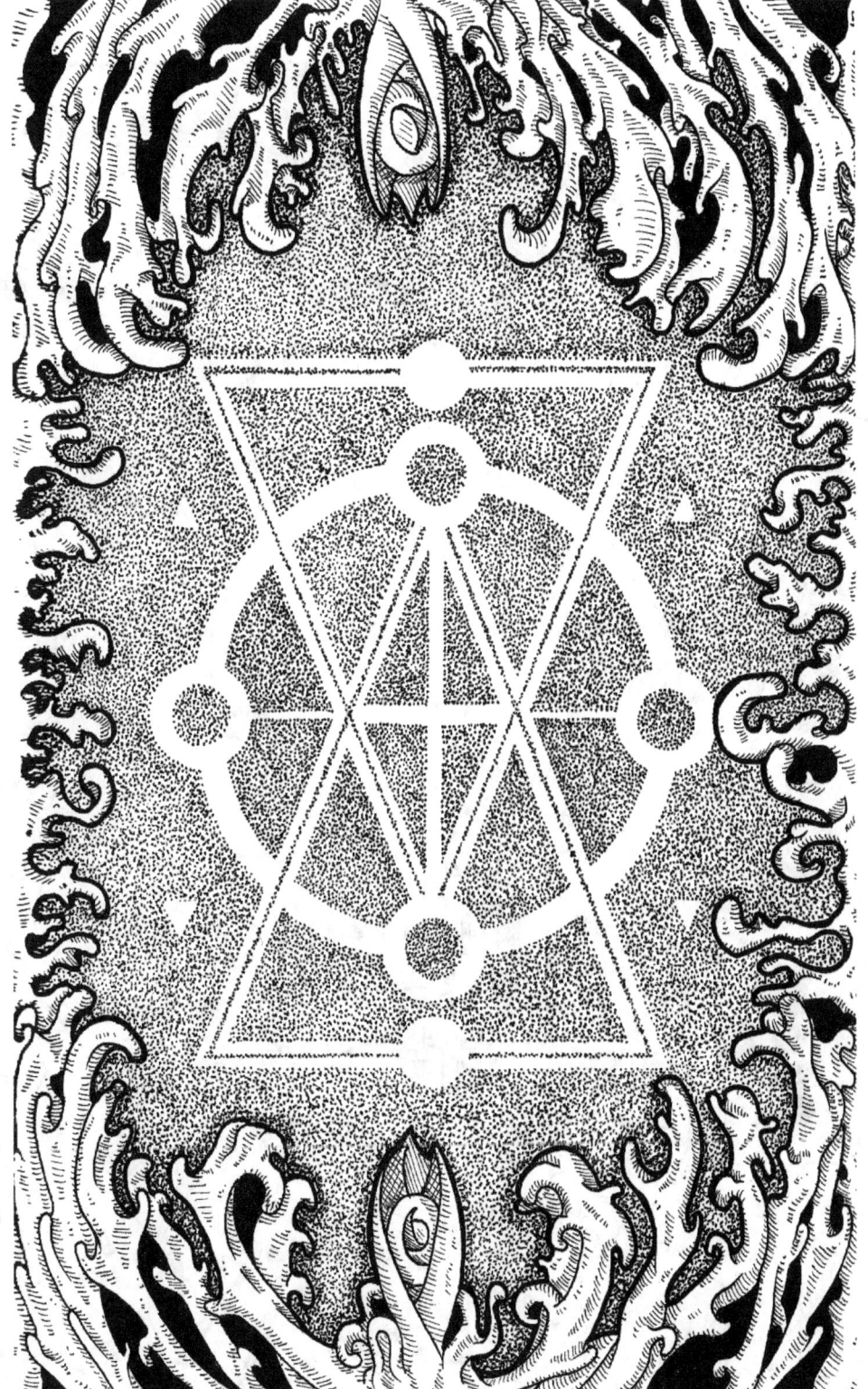

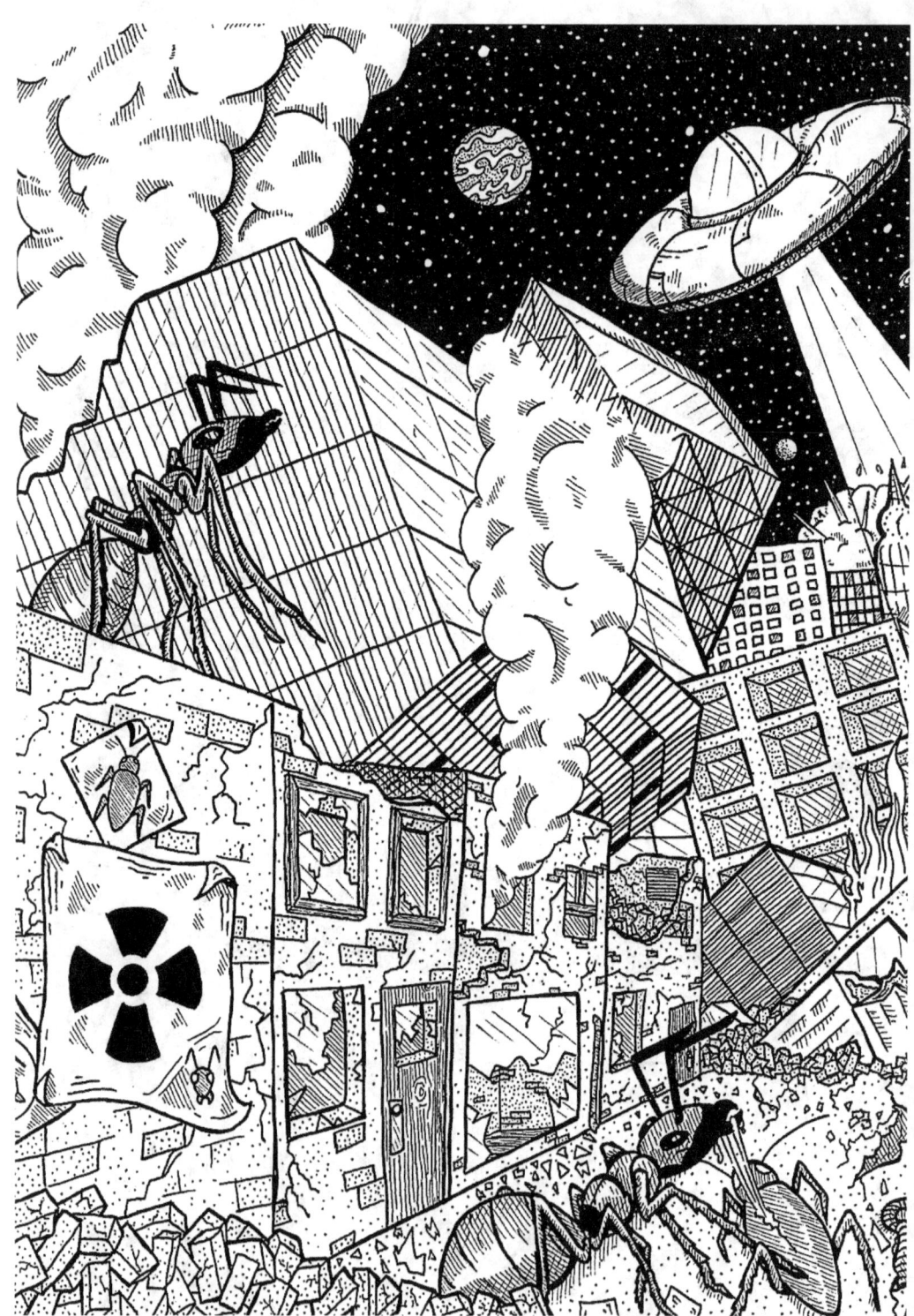

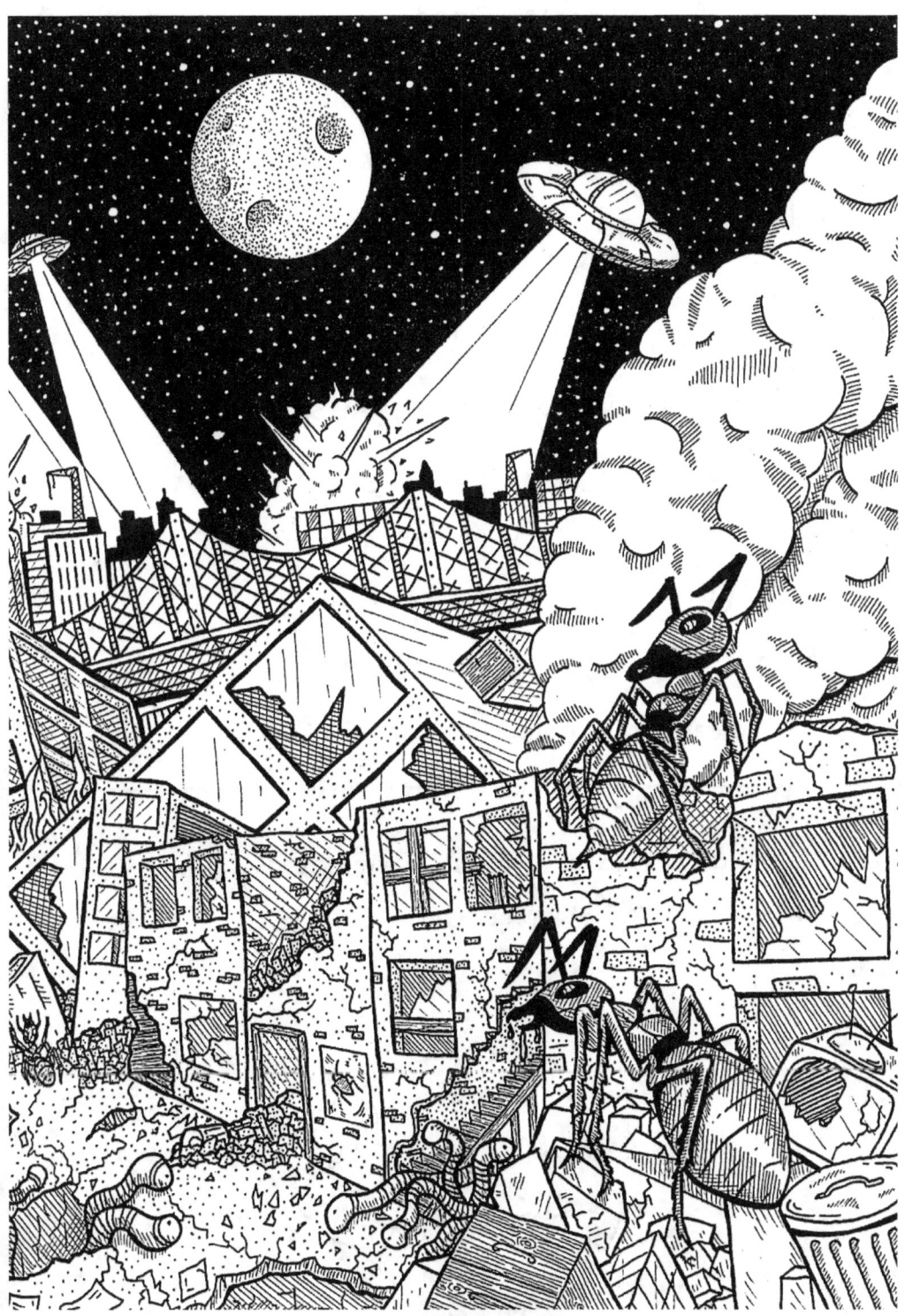

Little Seed...

This little seed so small and mute
Not square, nor round, not tree, nor fruit,

Not dressed in gold, no bells or horns
Potentials strewn out on the lawn,

What will you be, Where are you from,
Where will you go once you are gone?

A mighty oak free from the batch
A pumpkin in a pumpkin patch,

Will this seed expand my mind
And leave my ego far behind,

Or meet it's end with no inflations
Failed by natures cruel mutations,

I guess that you will never know
What's never planted will not grow.

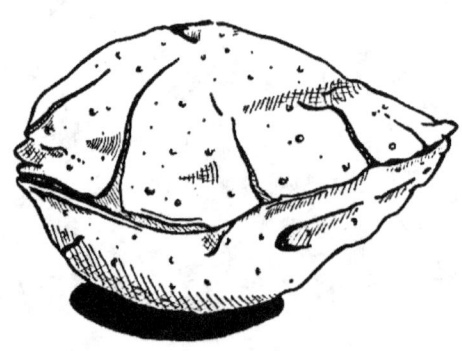

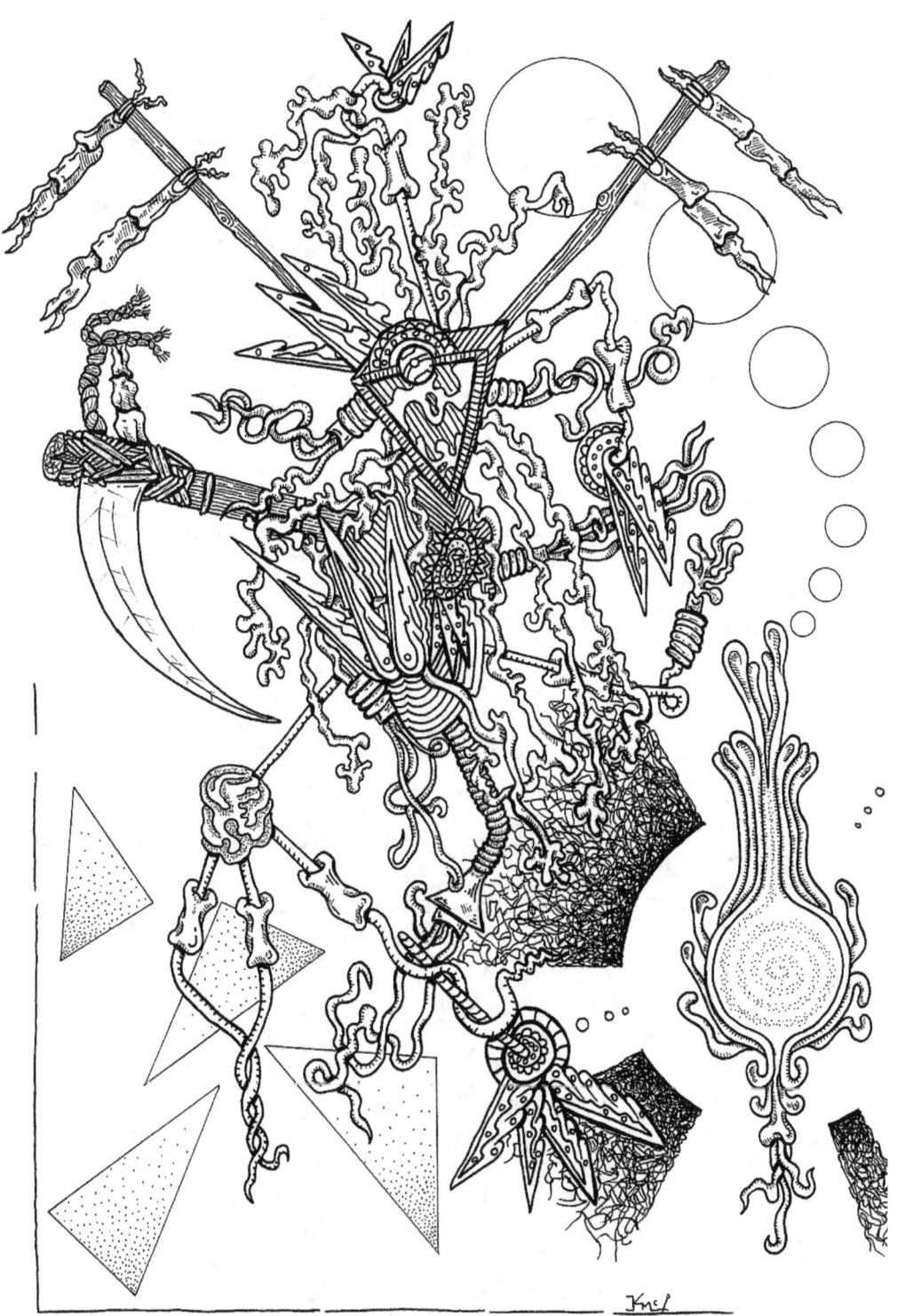

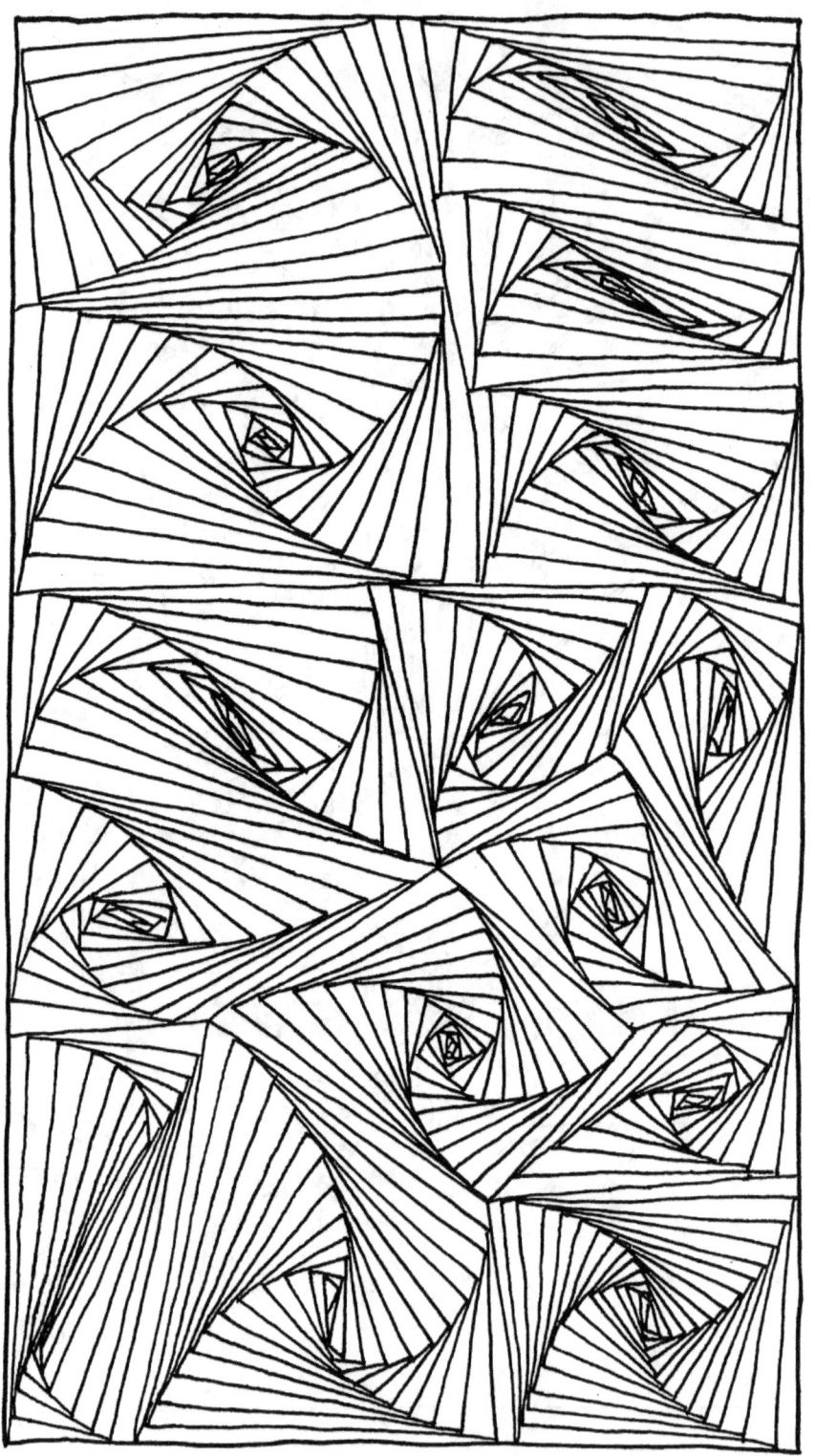

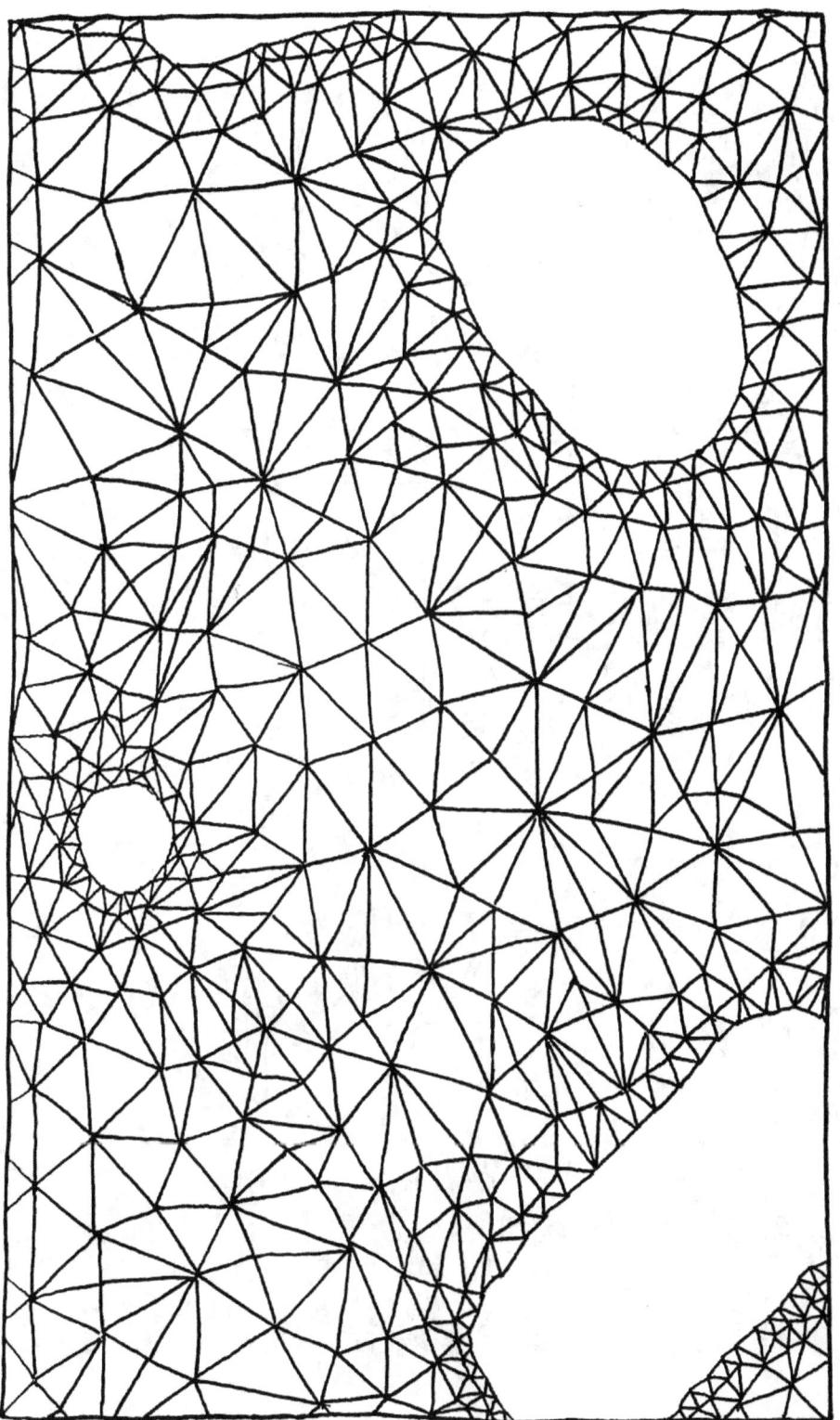

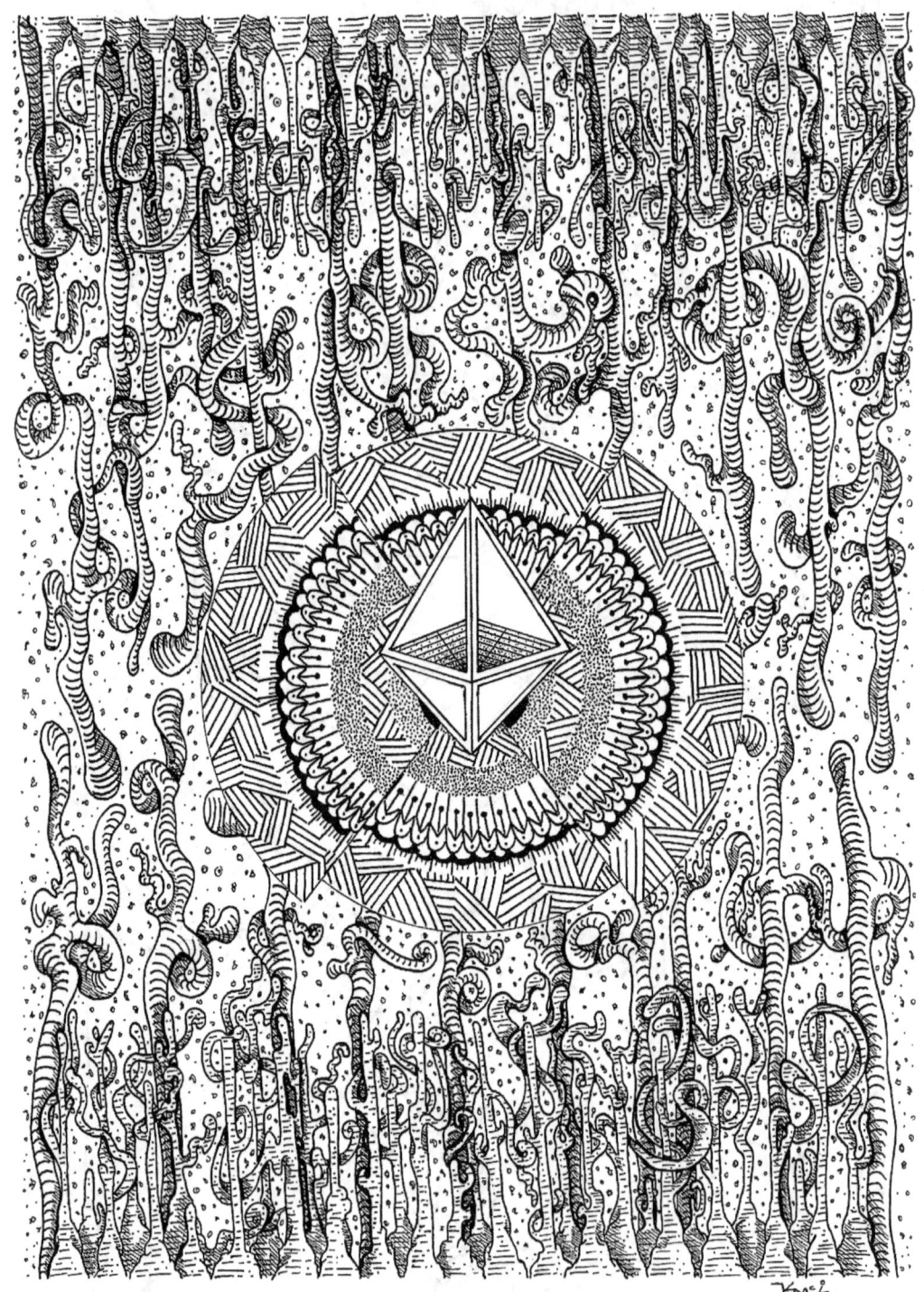

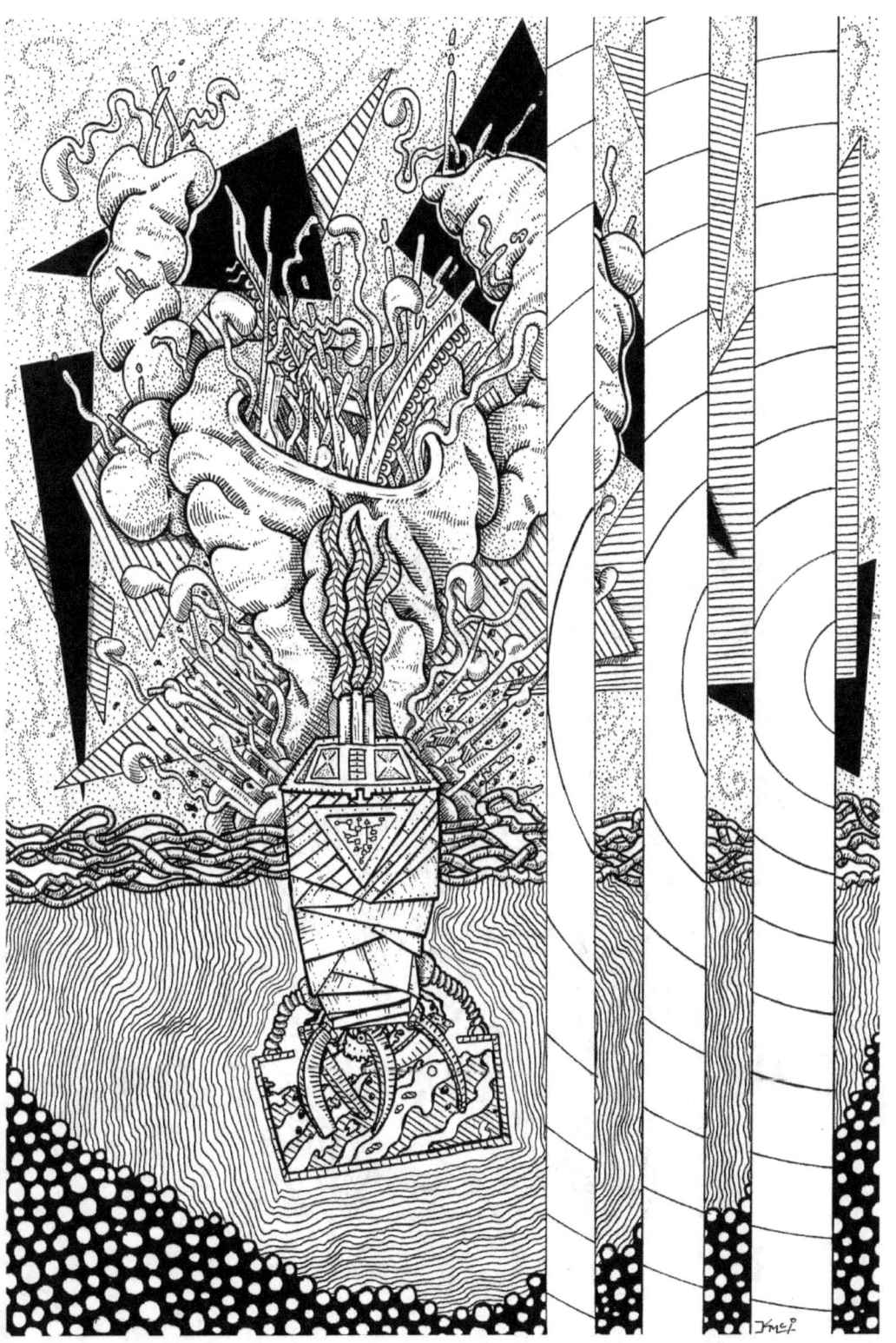

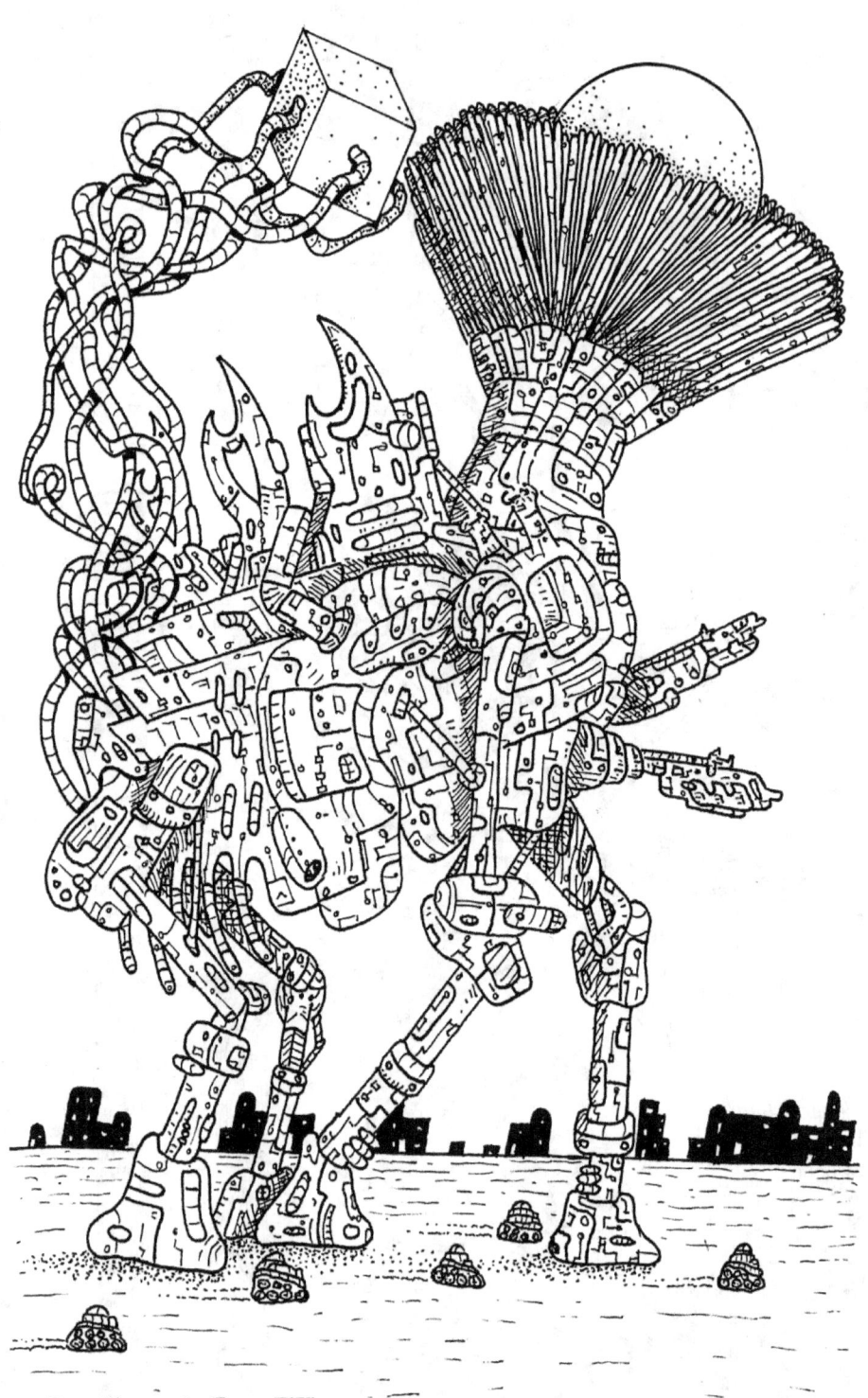

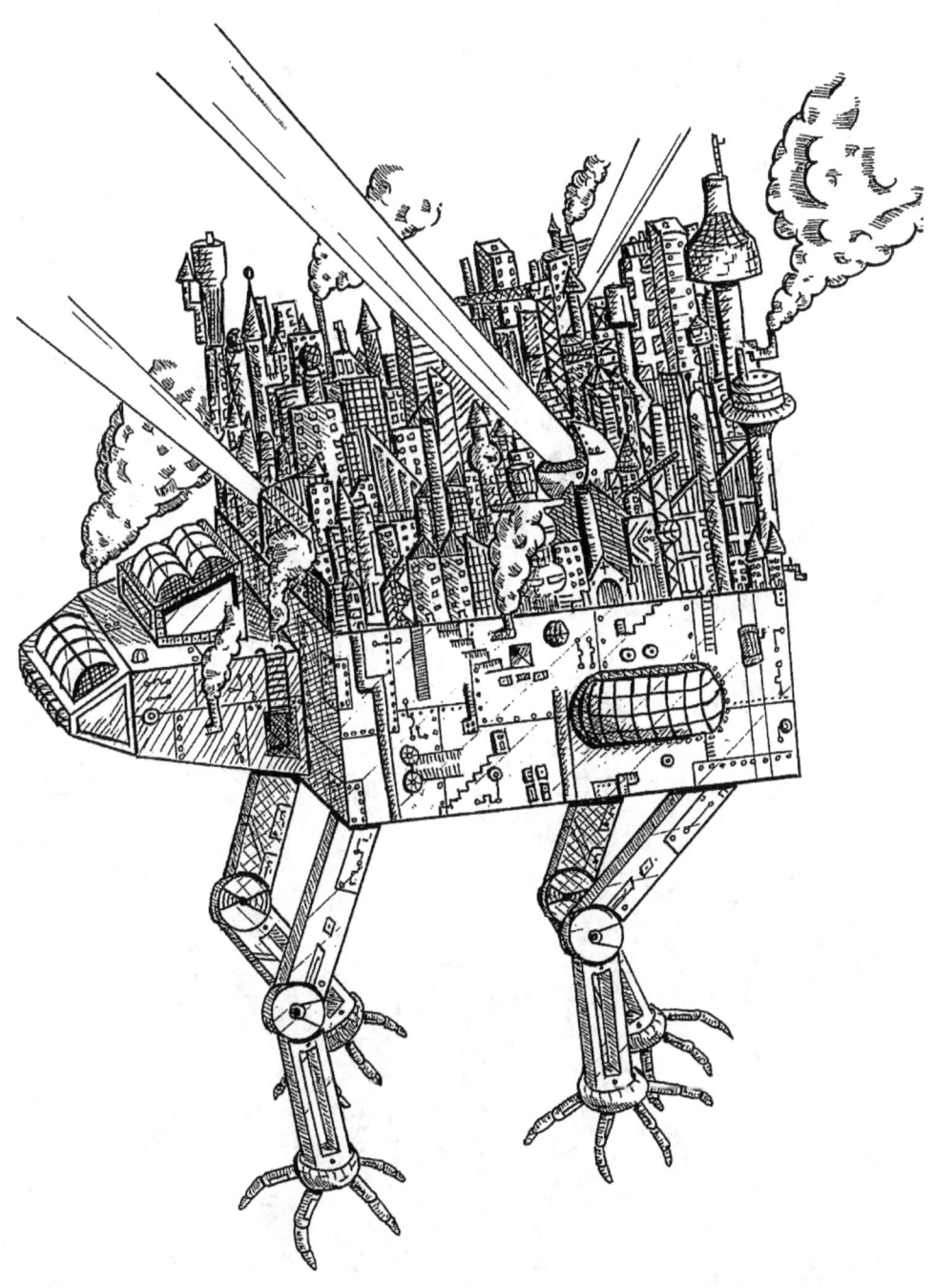

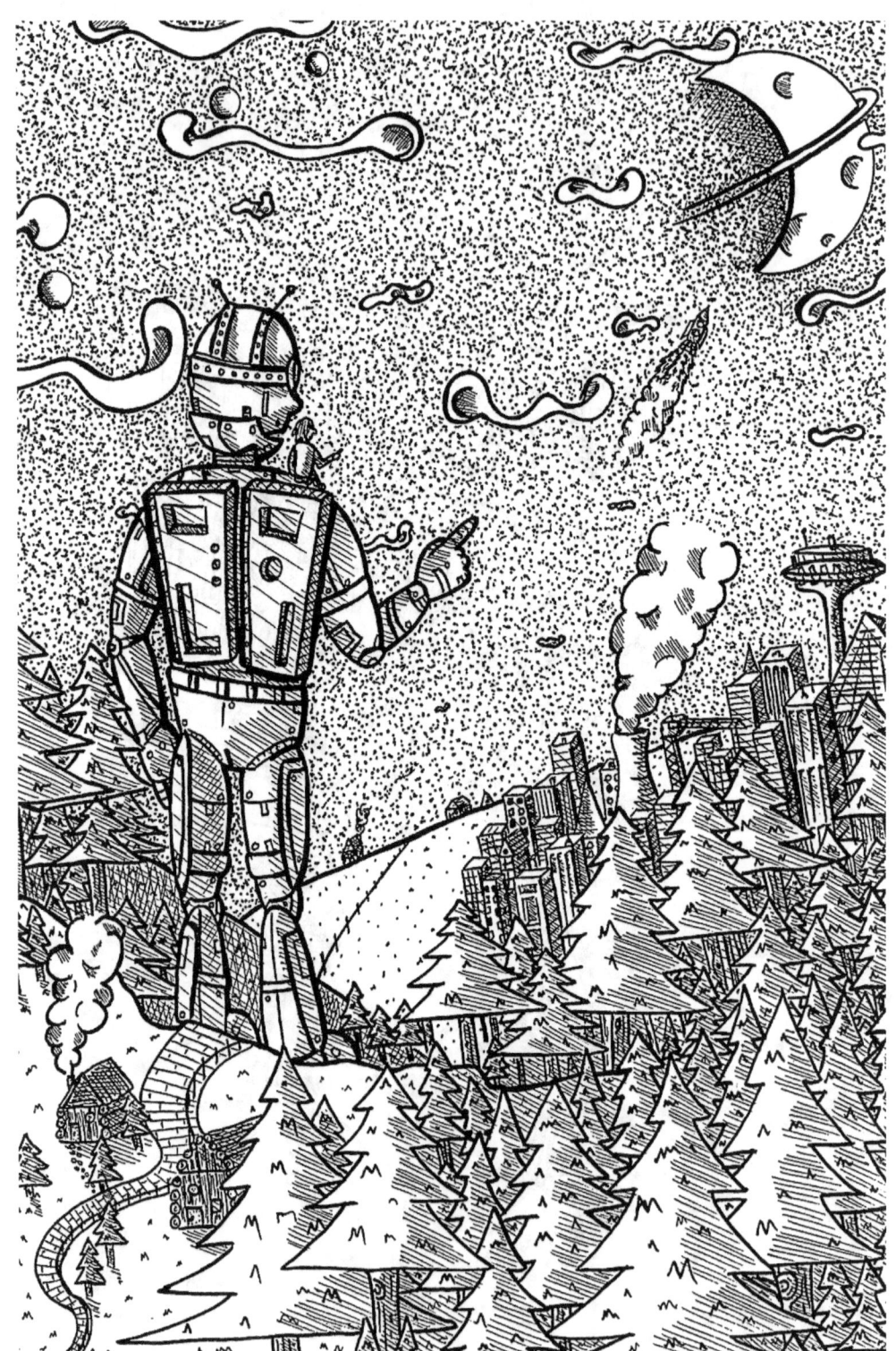

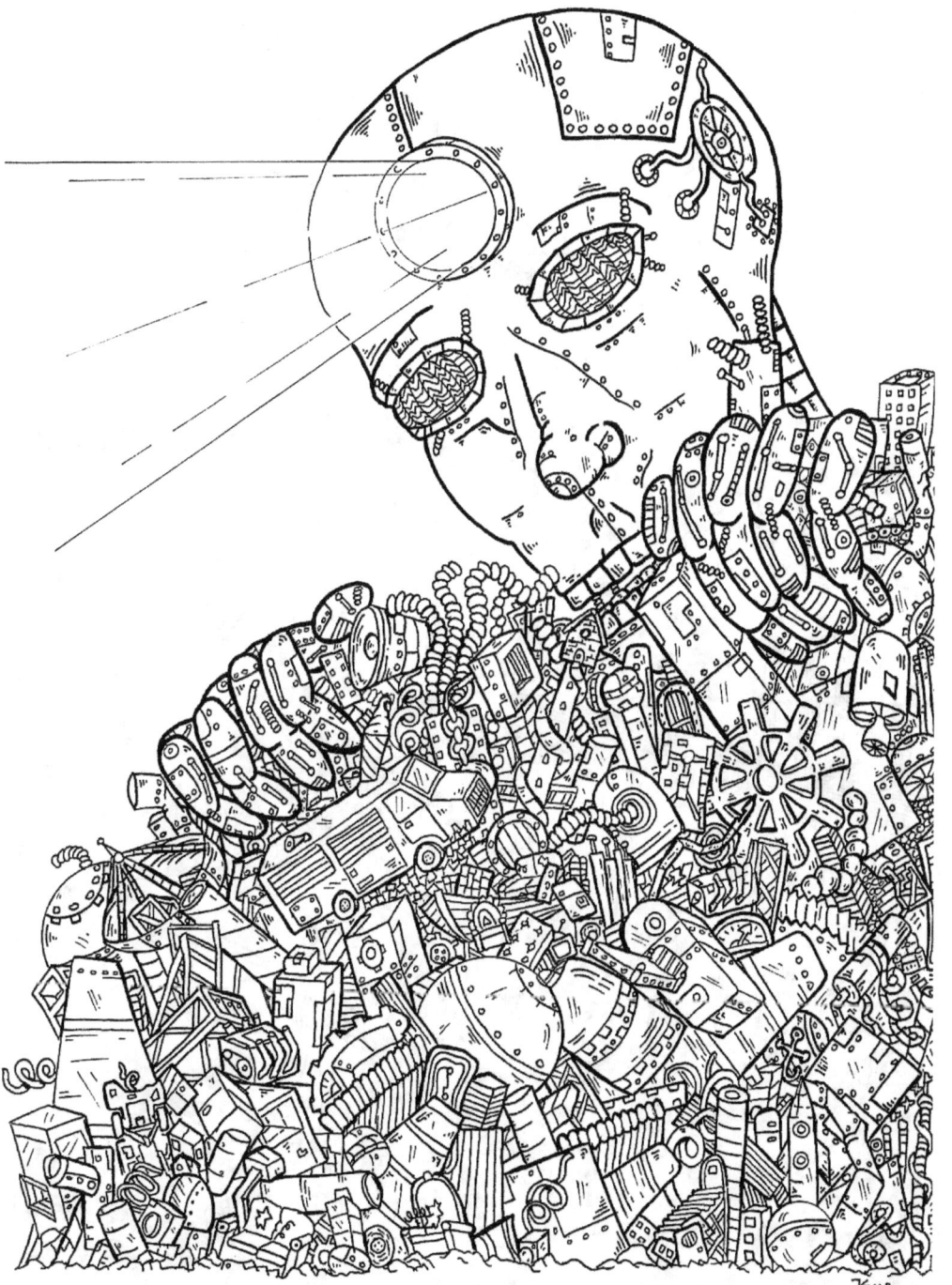

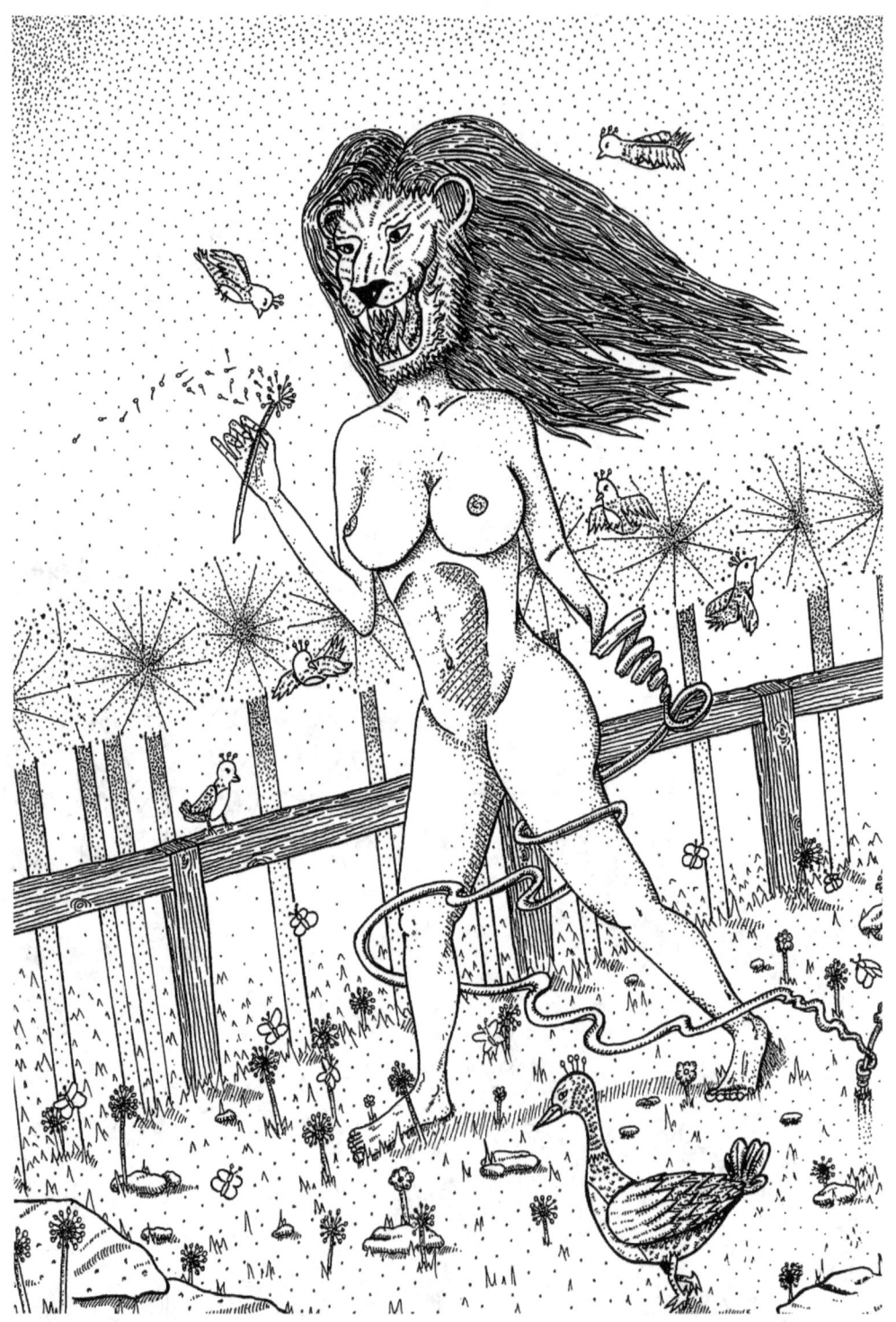

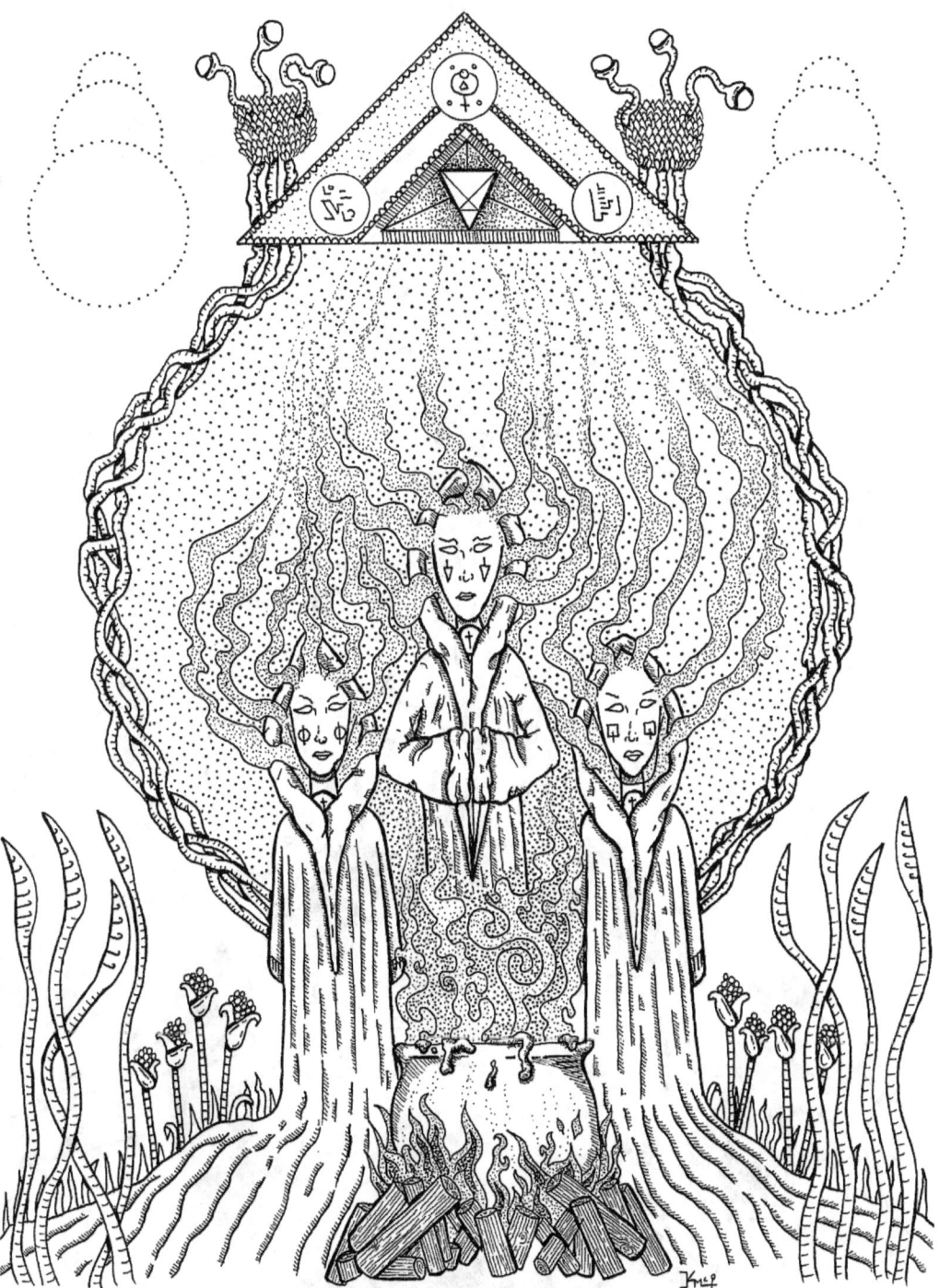

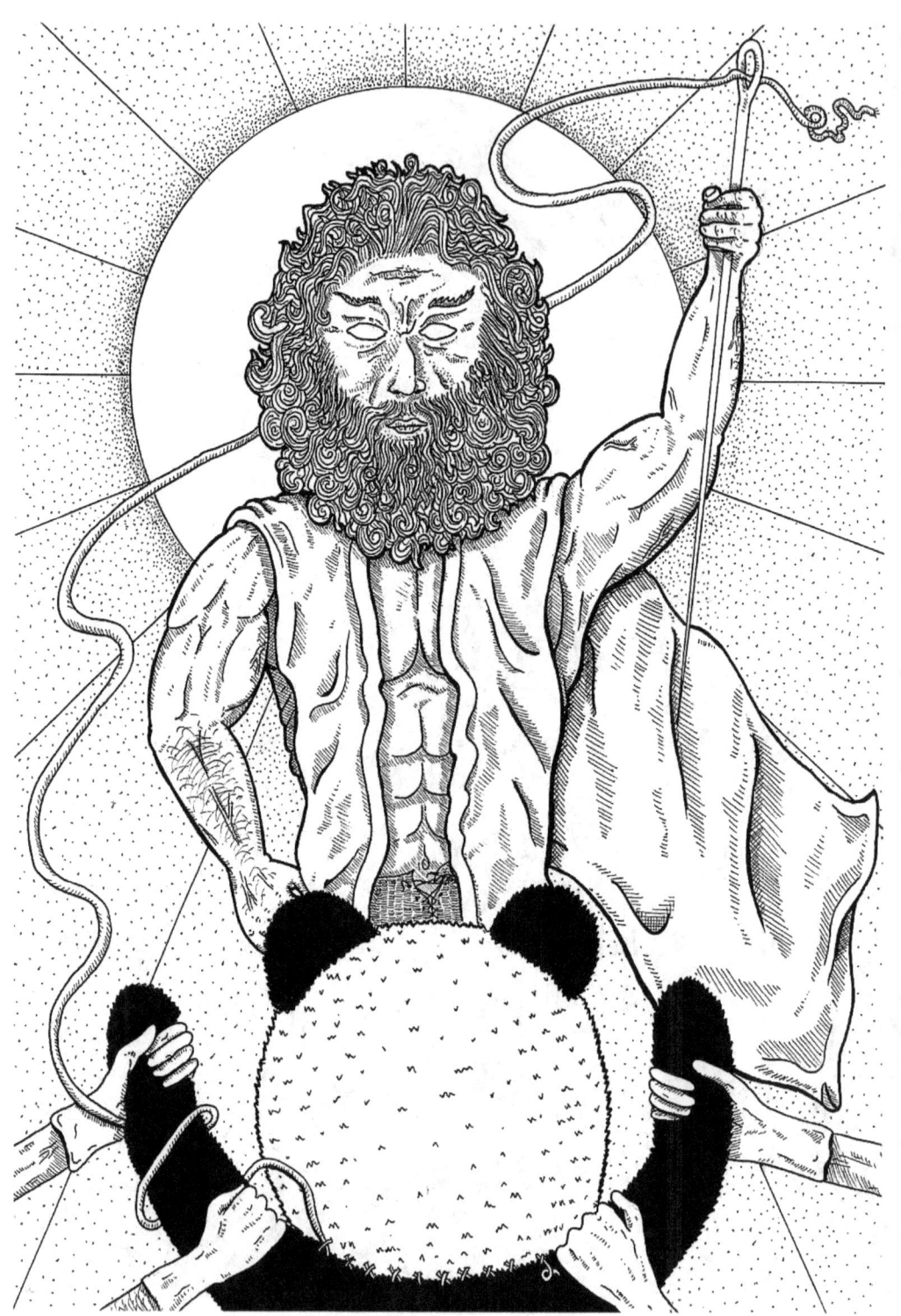

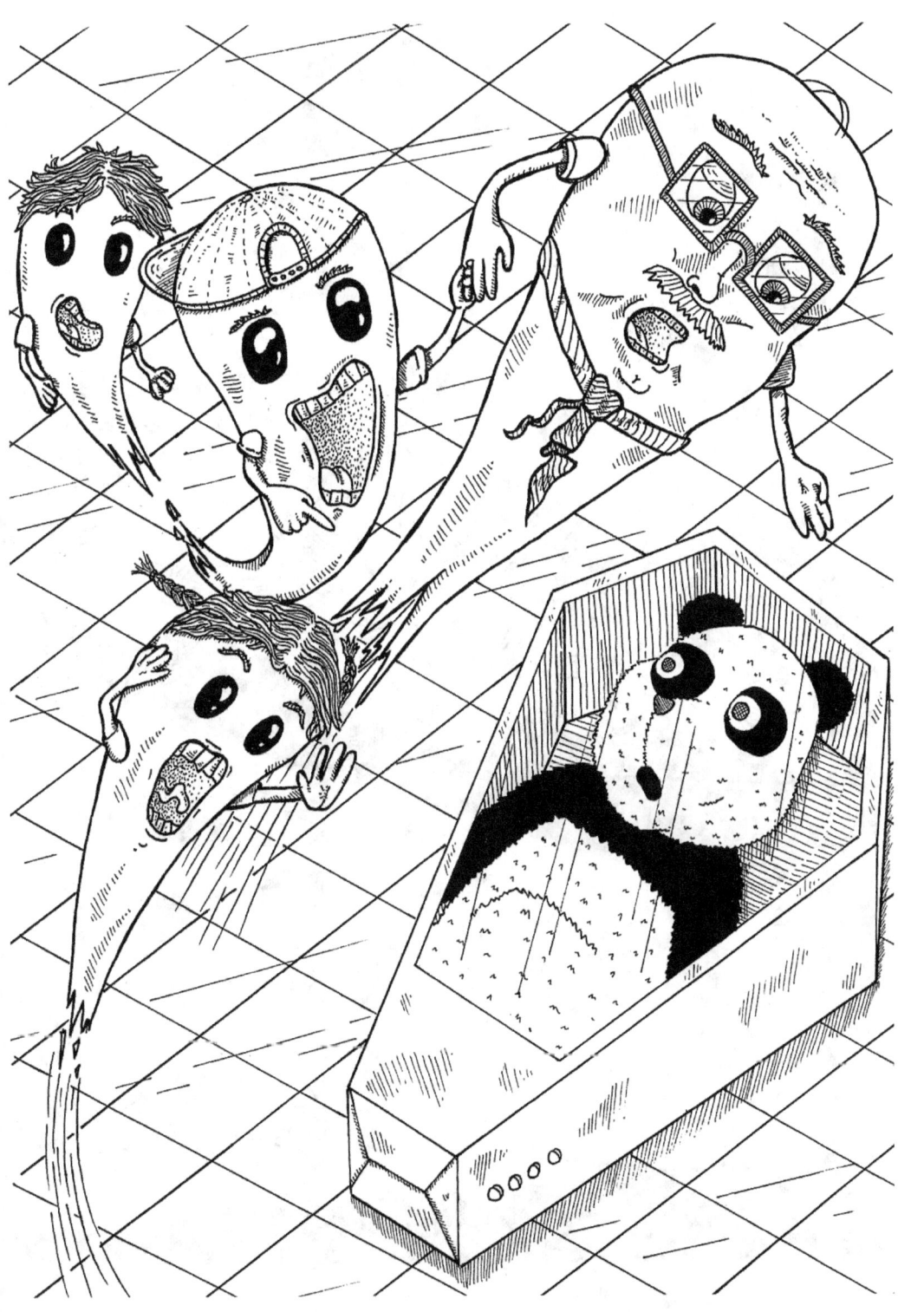

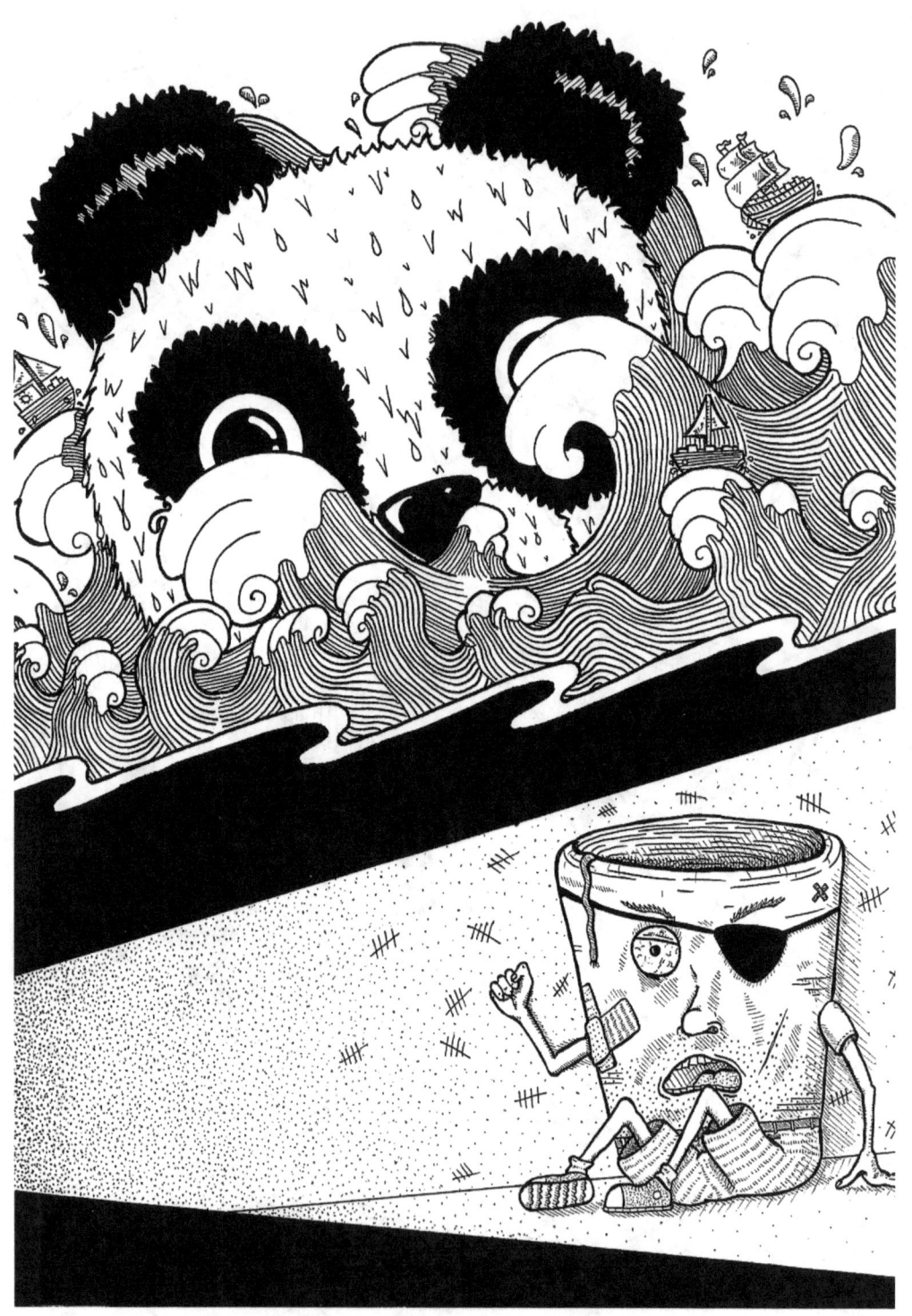

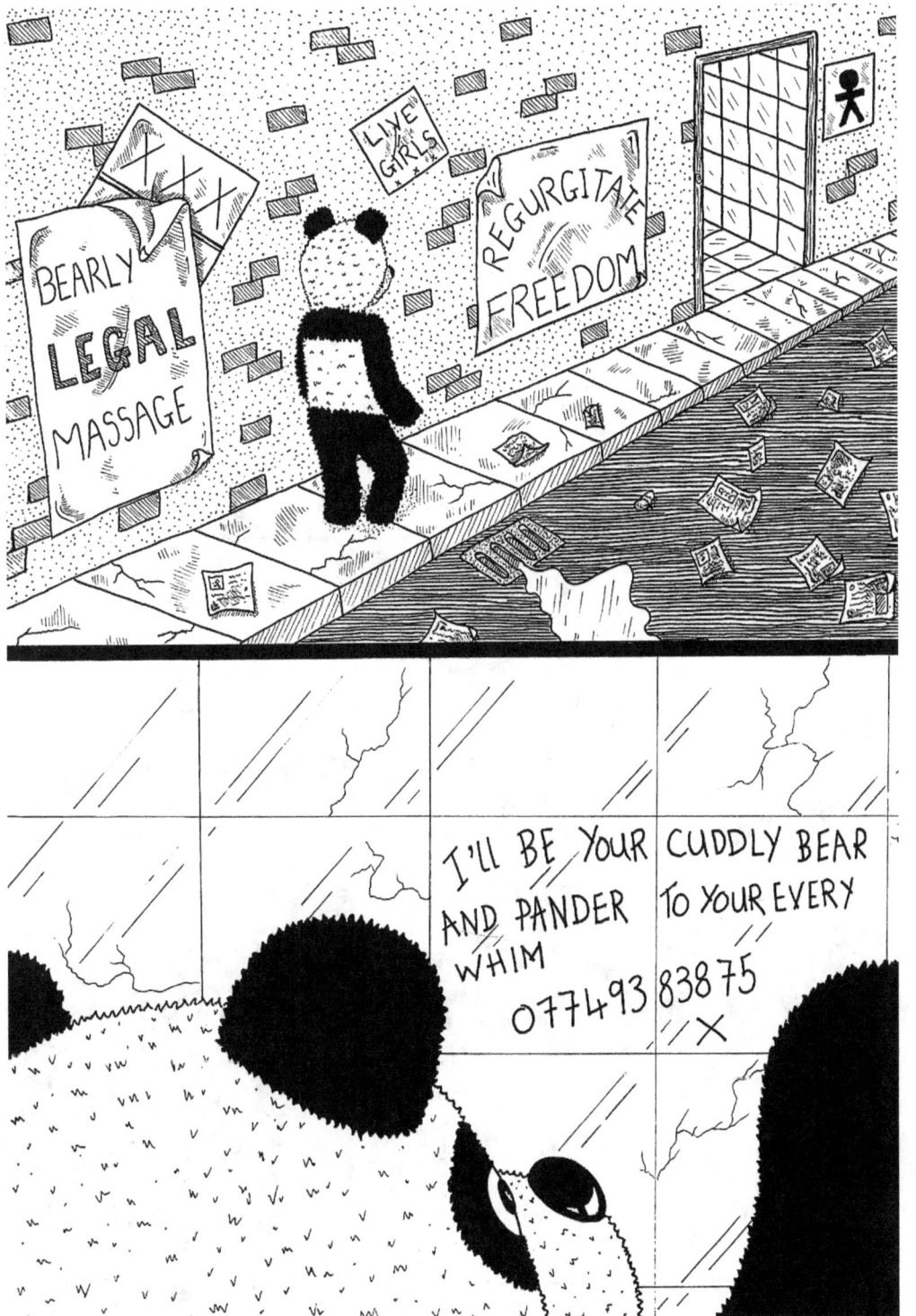

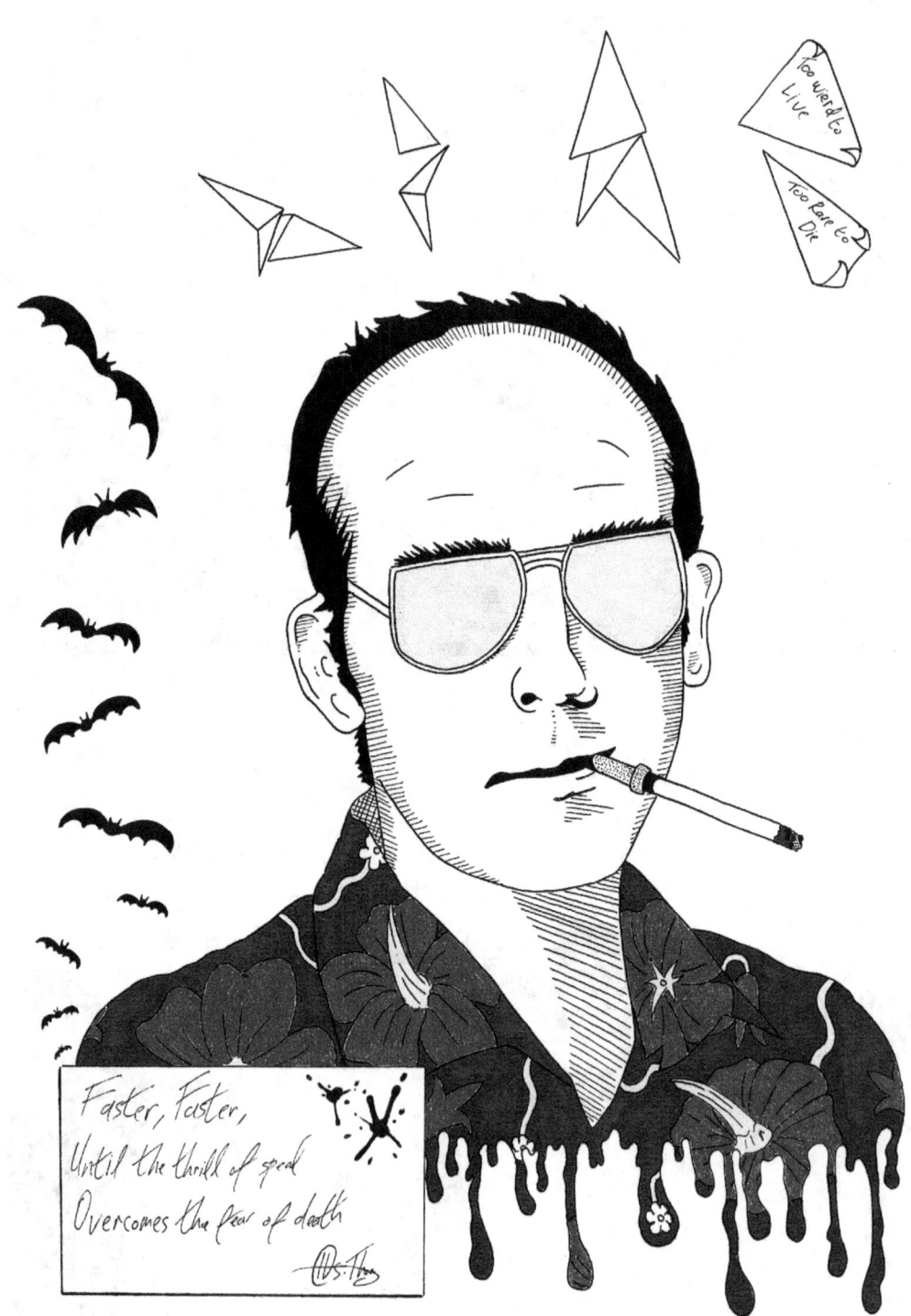

Too weird to Live

Too Rare to Die

Faster, Faster,
Until the thrill of speed
Overcomes the fear of death

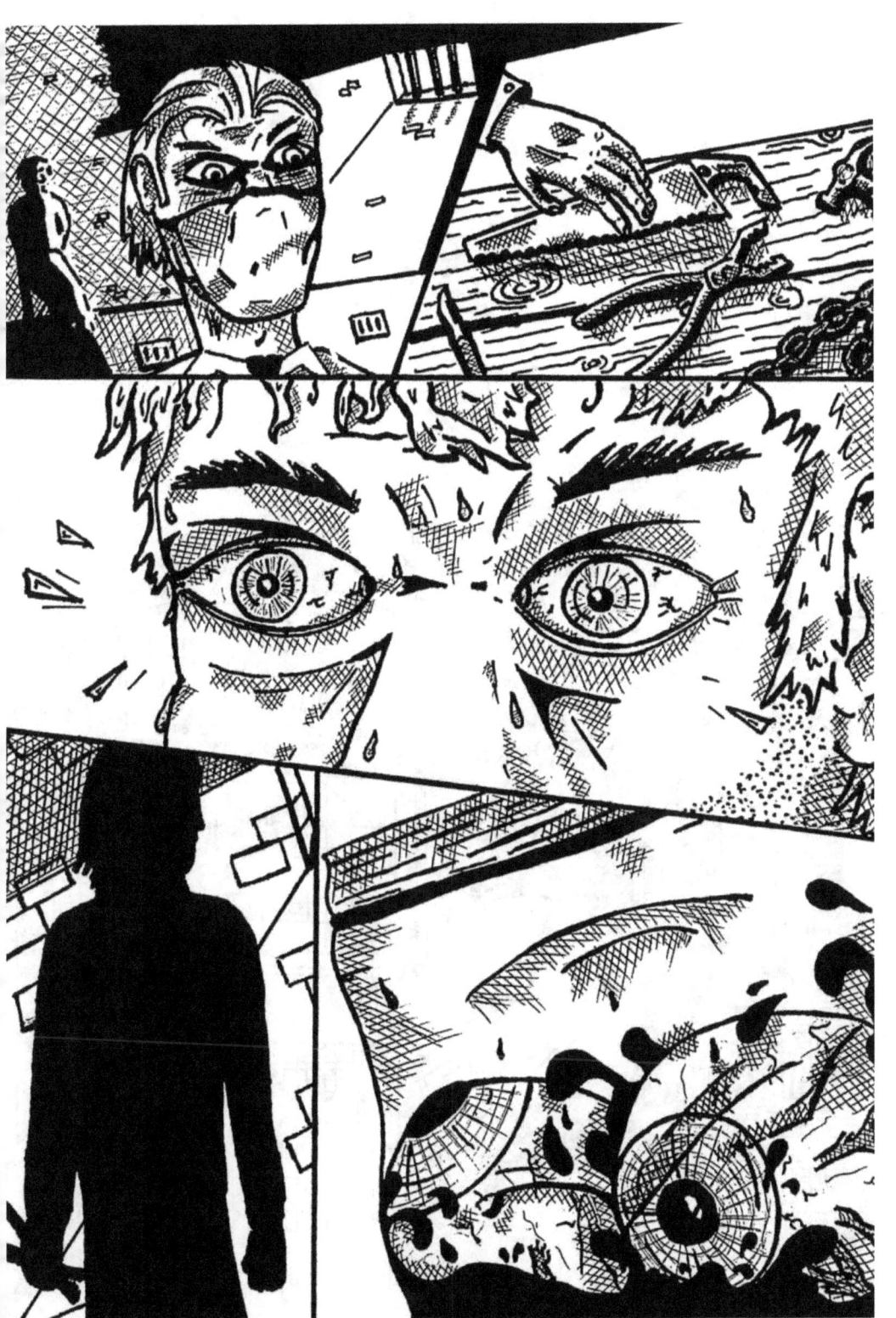

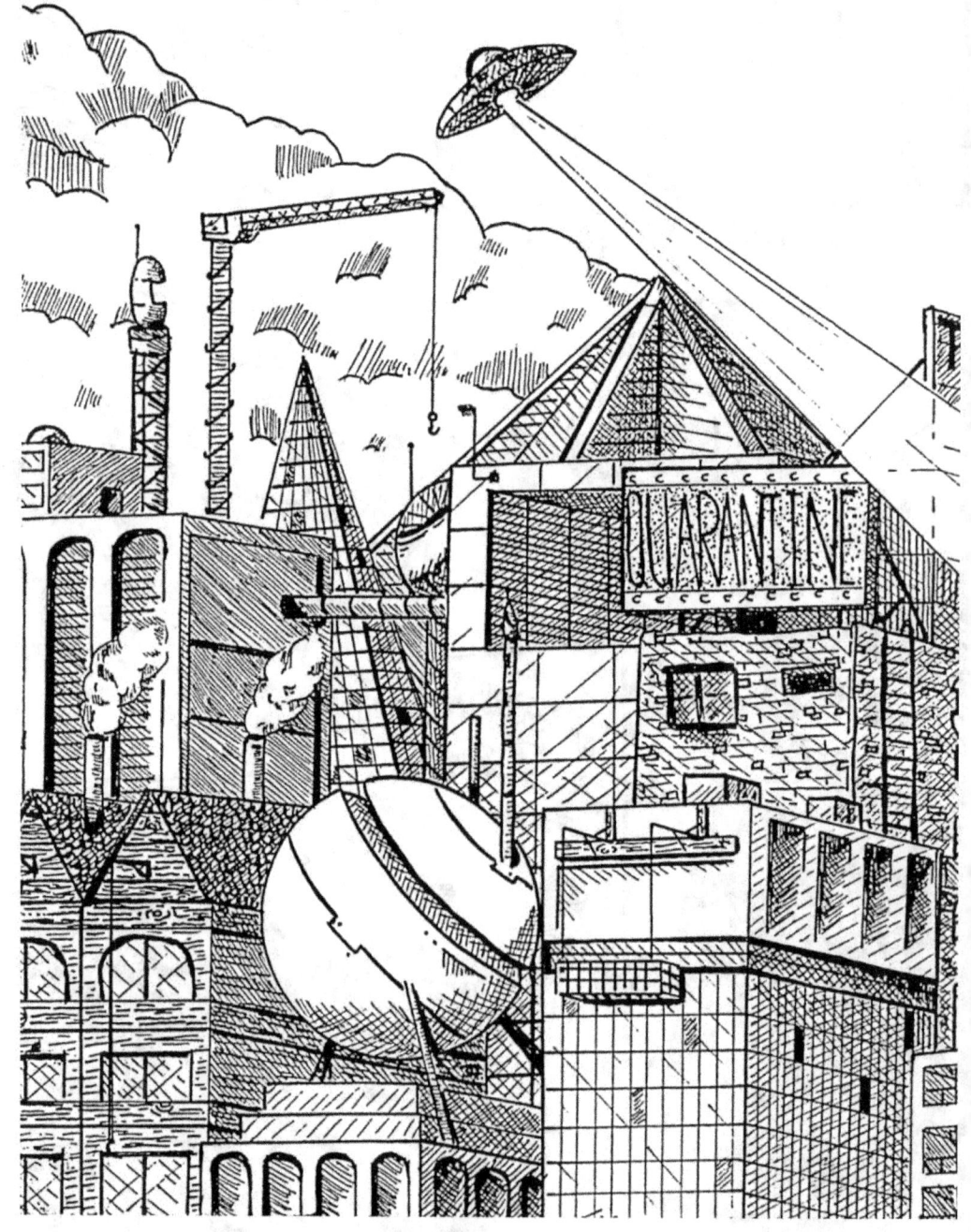

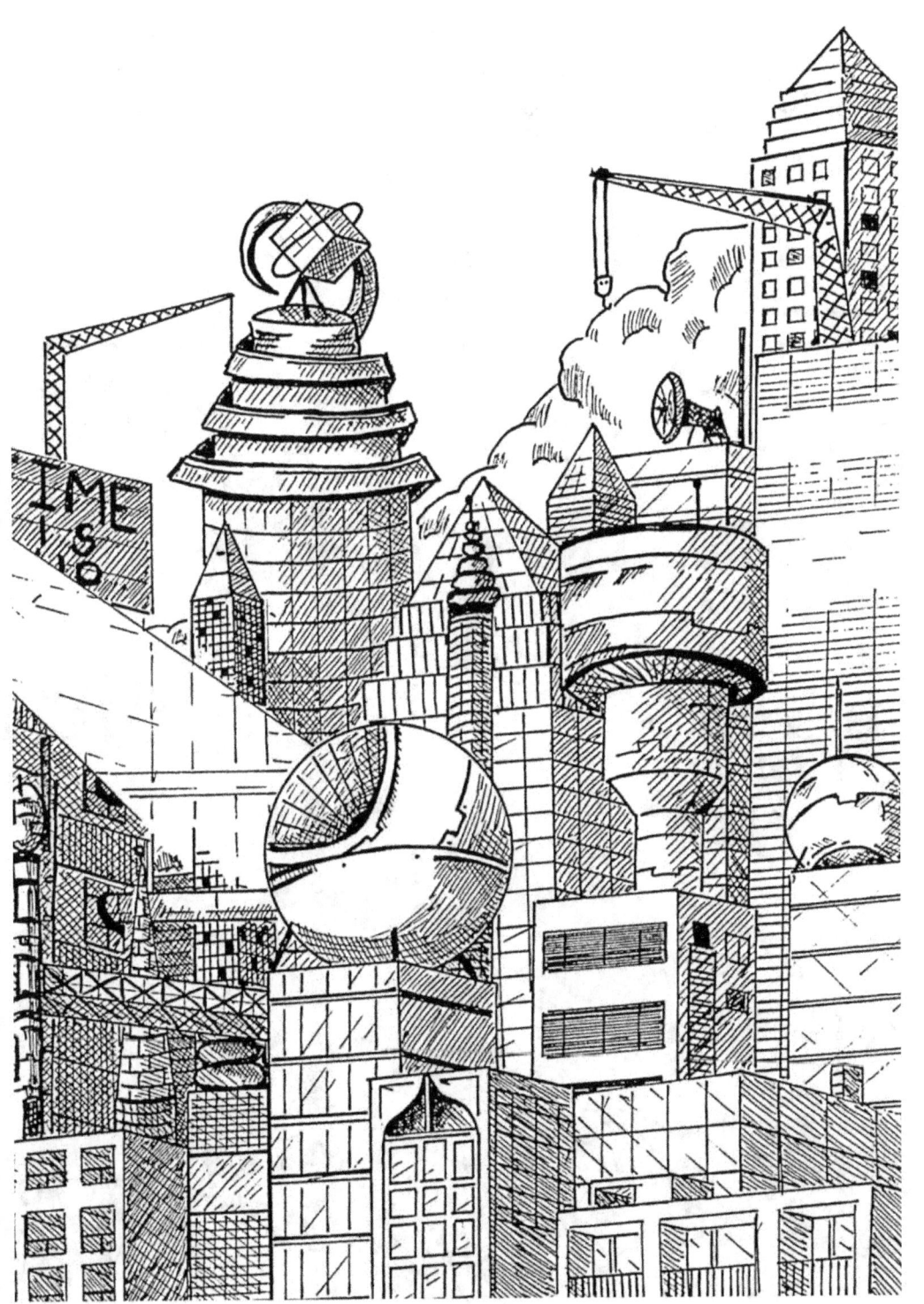

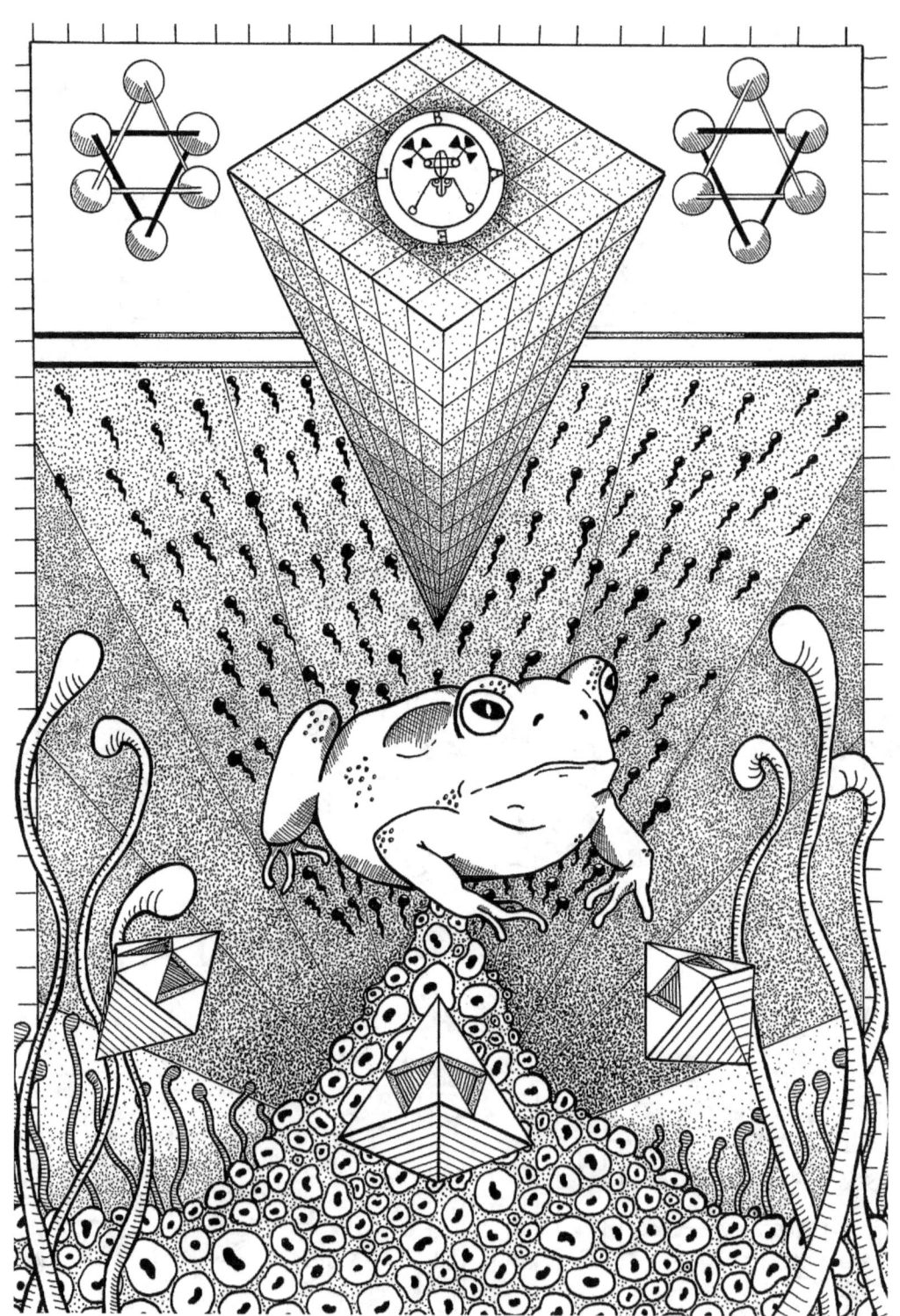

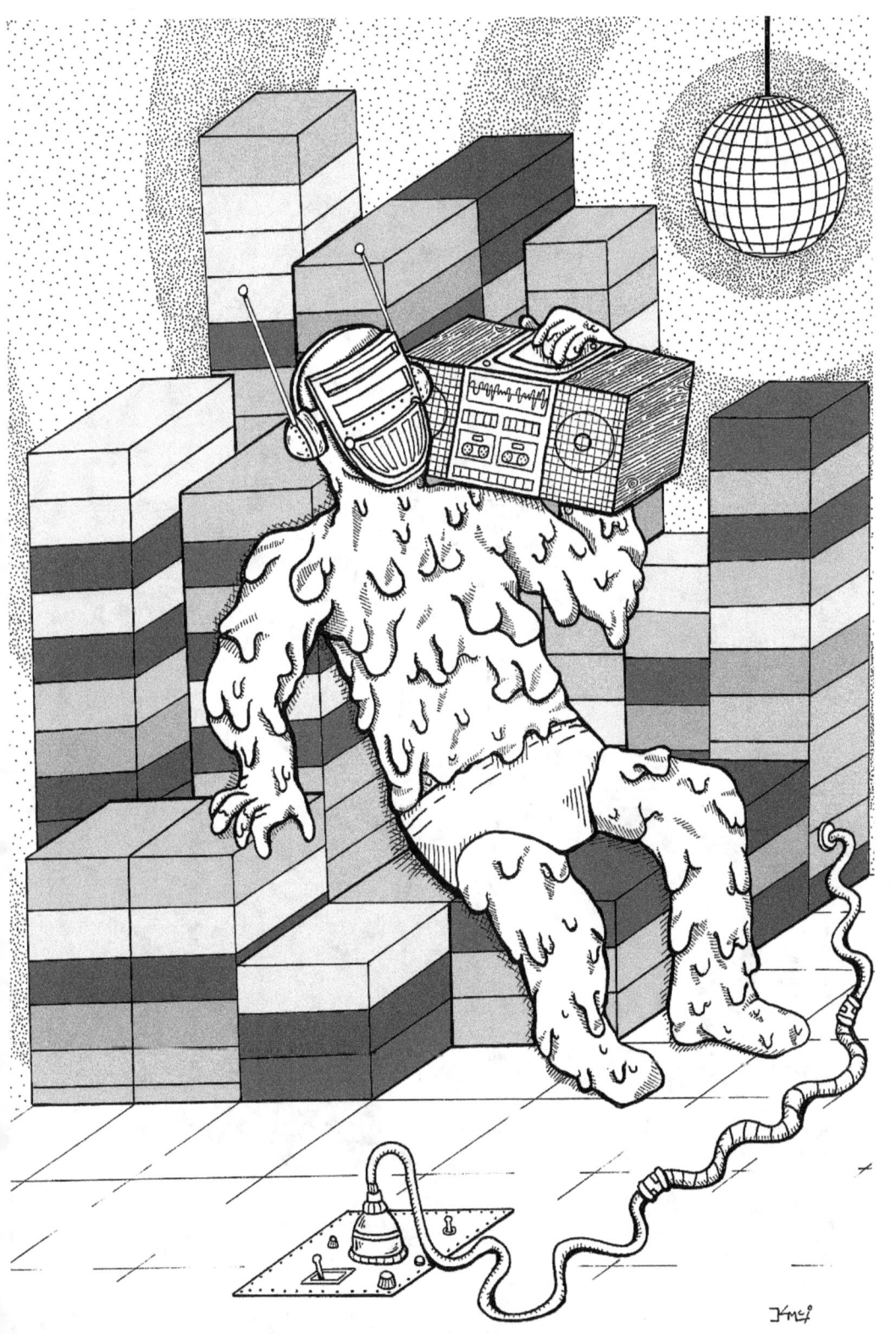

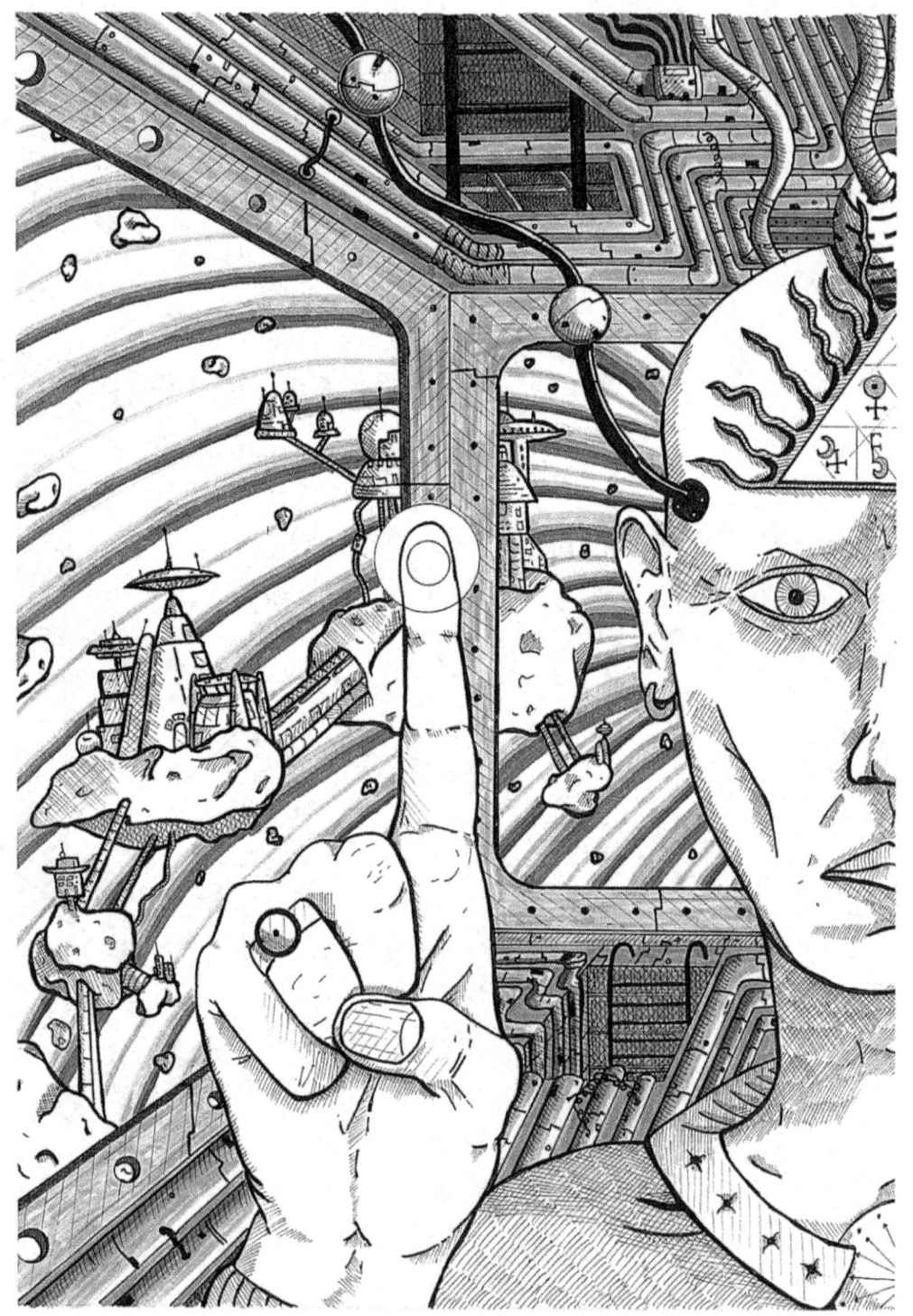

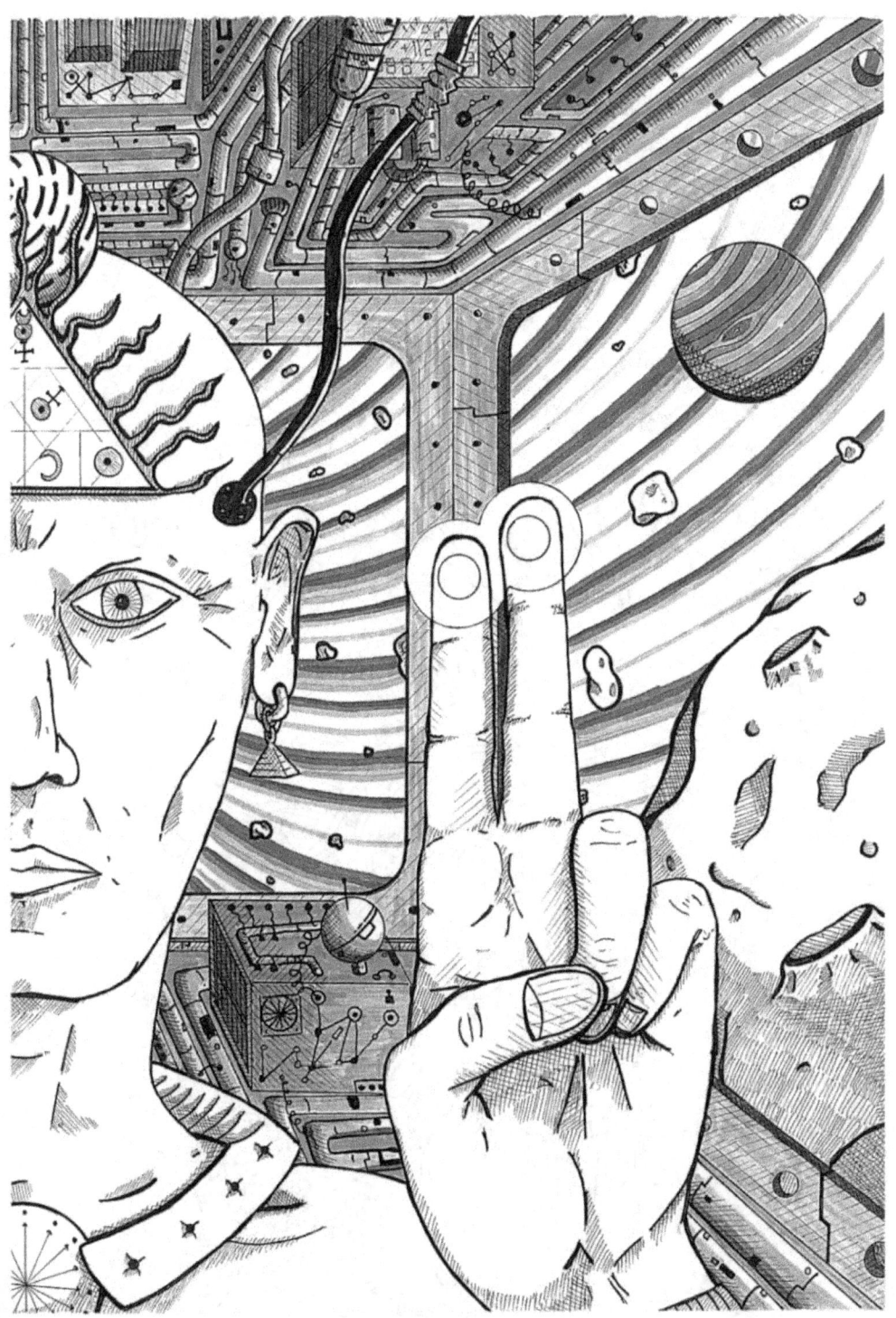

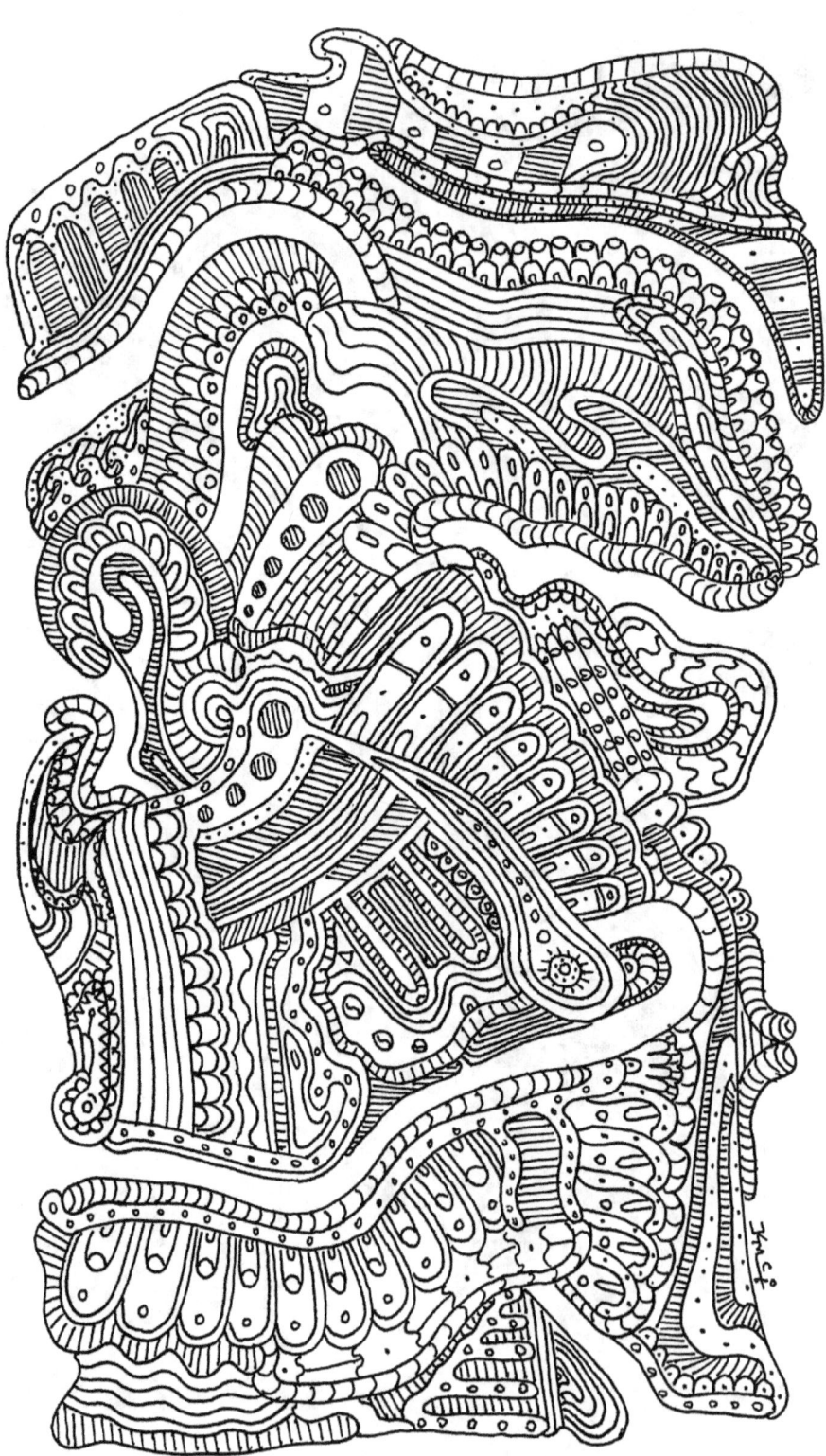

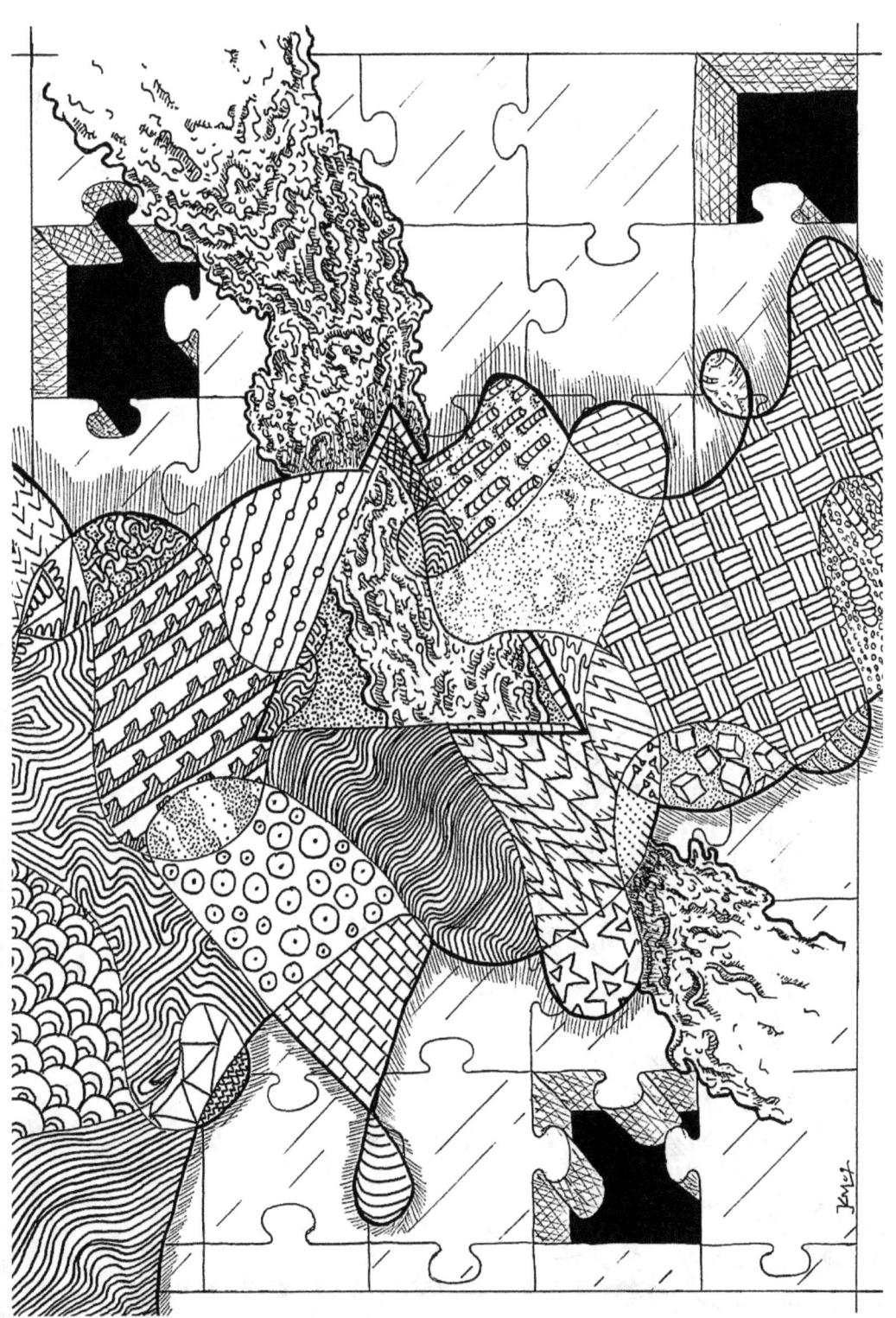

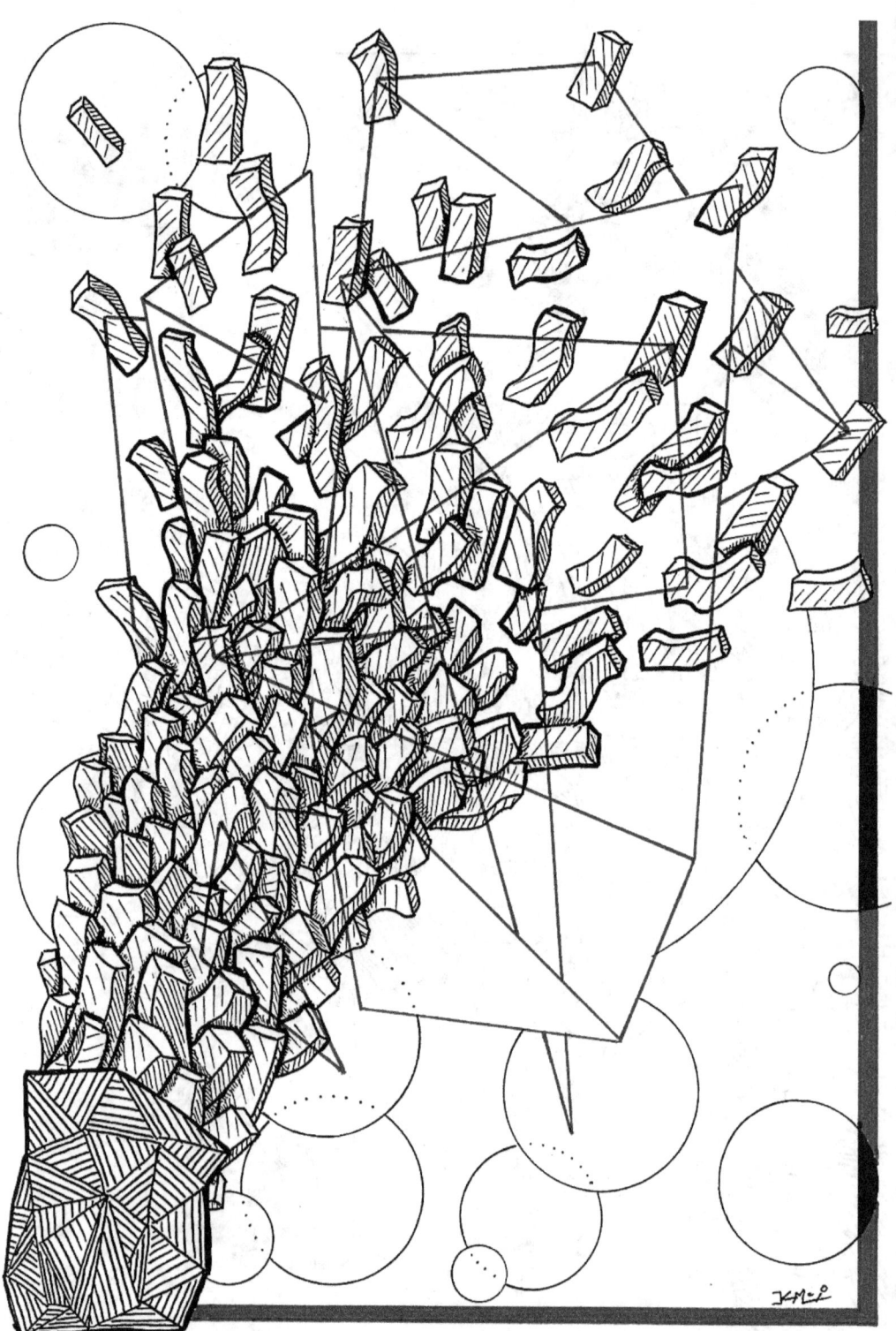

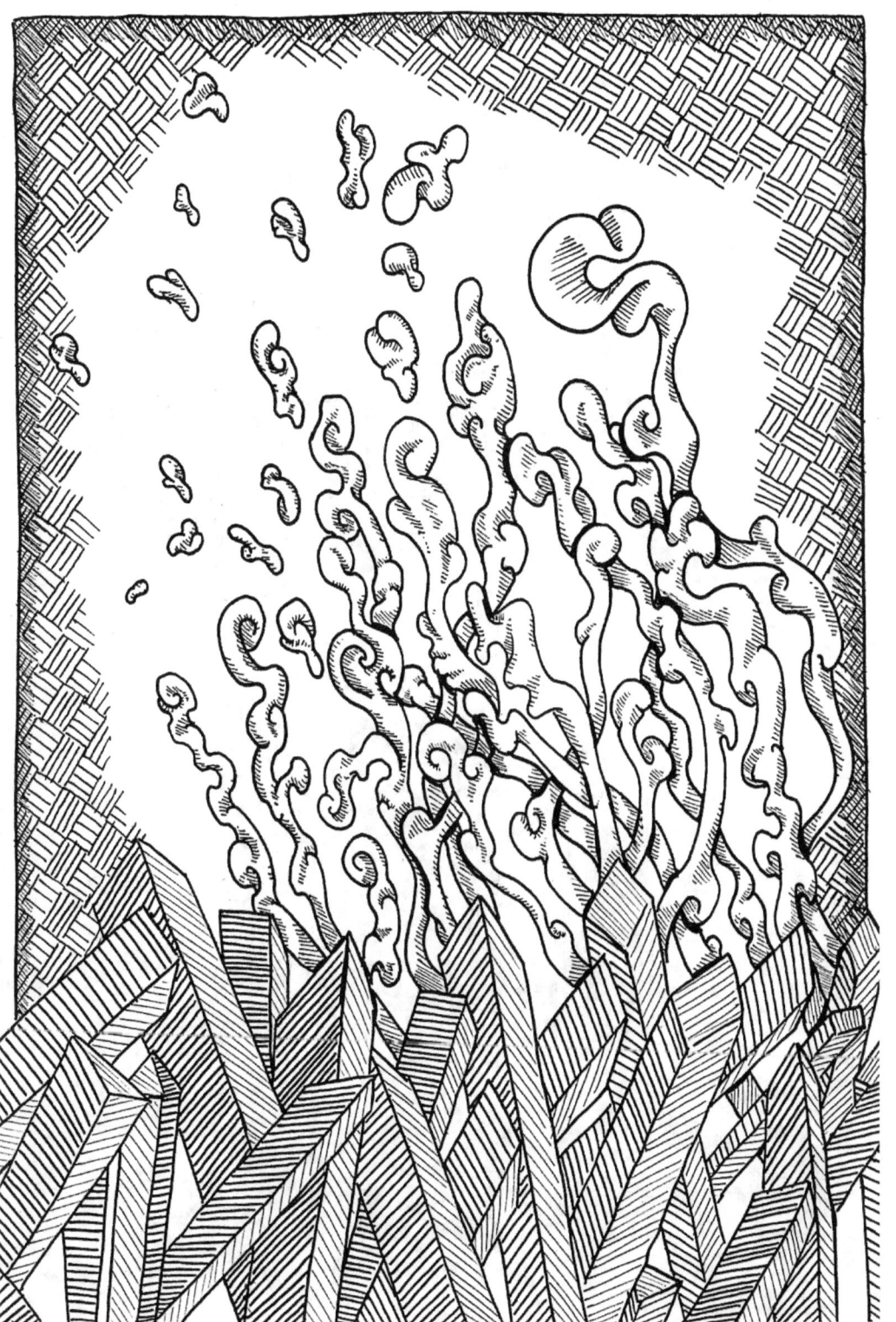

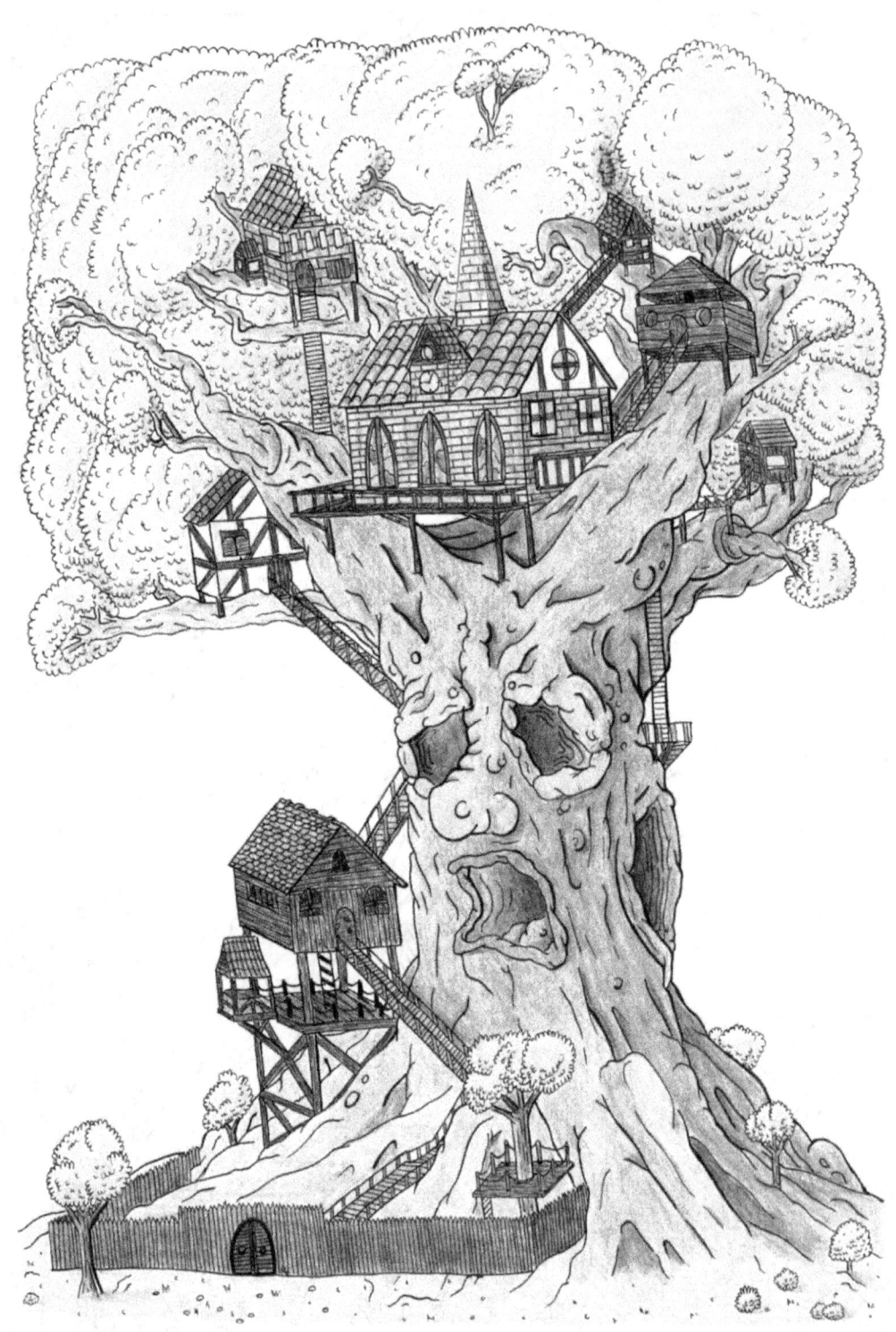

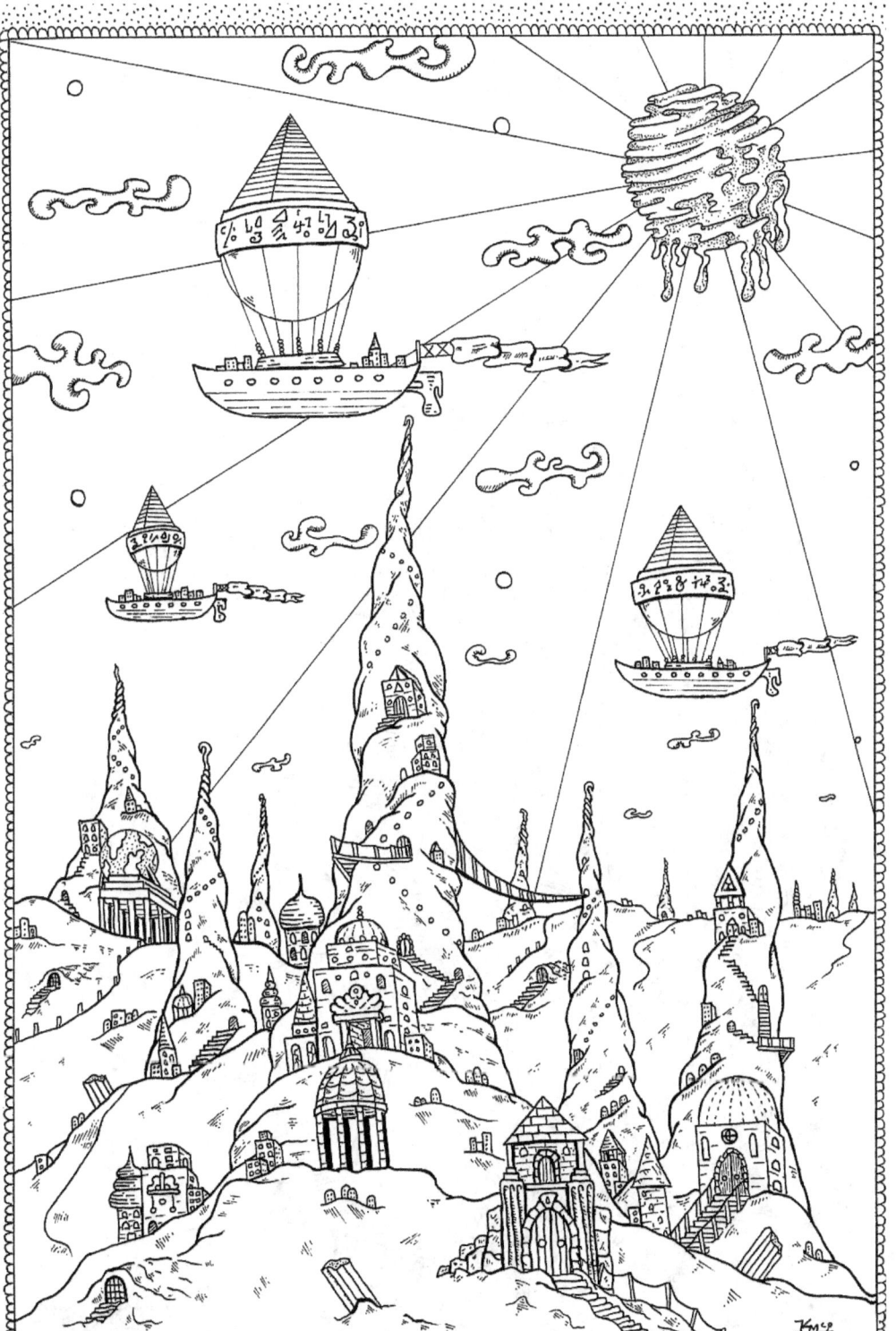

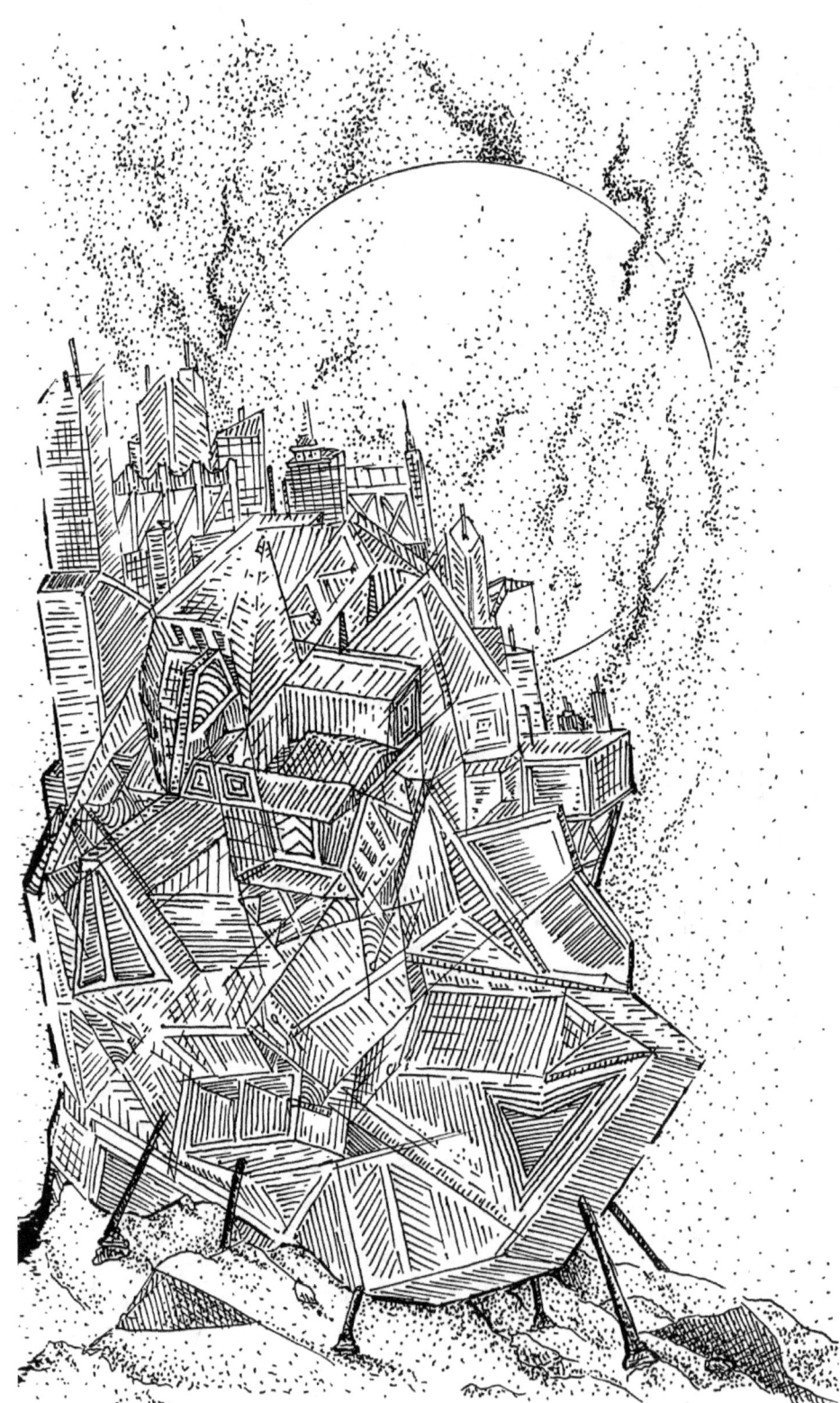

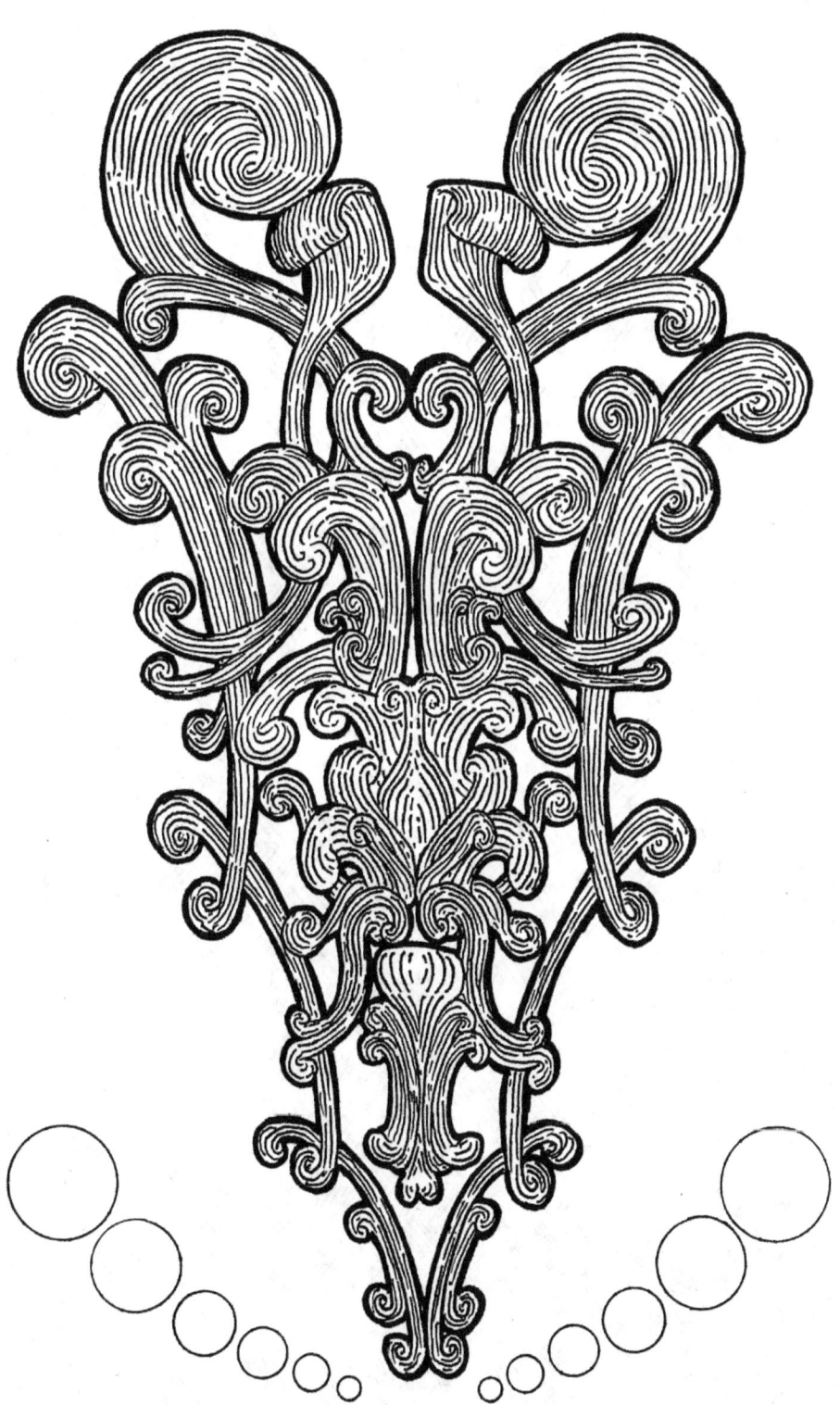

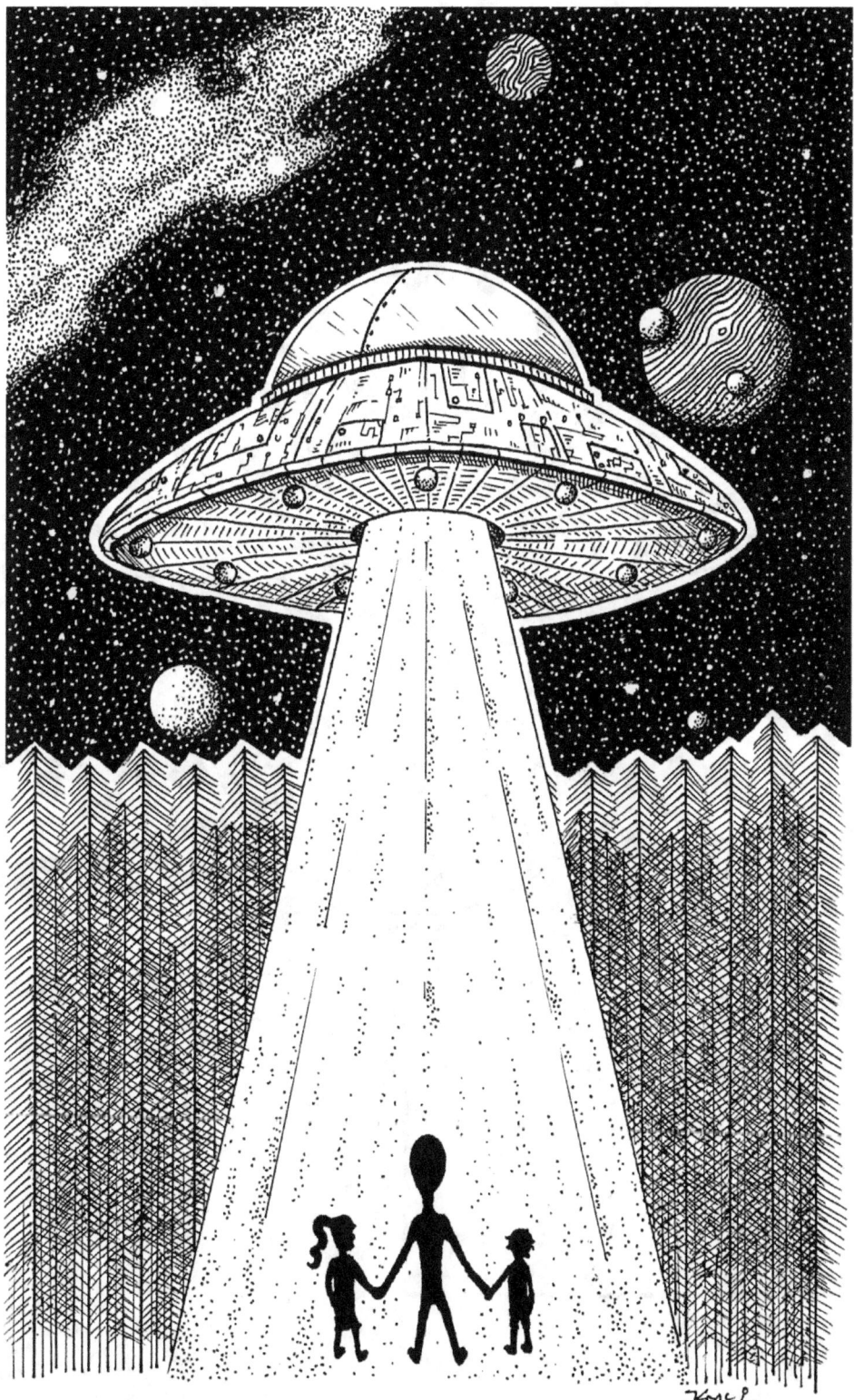

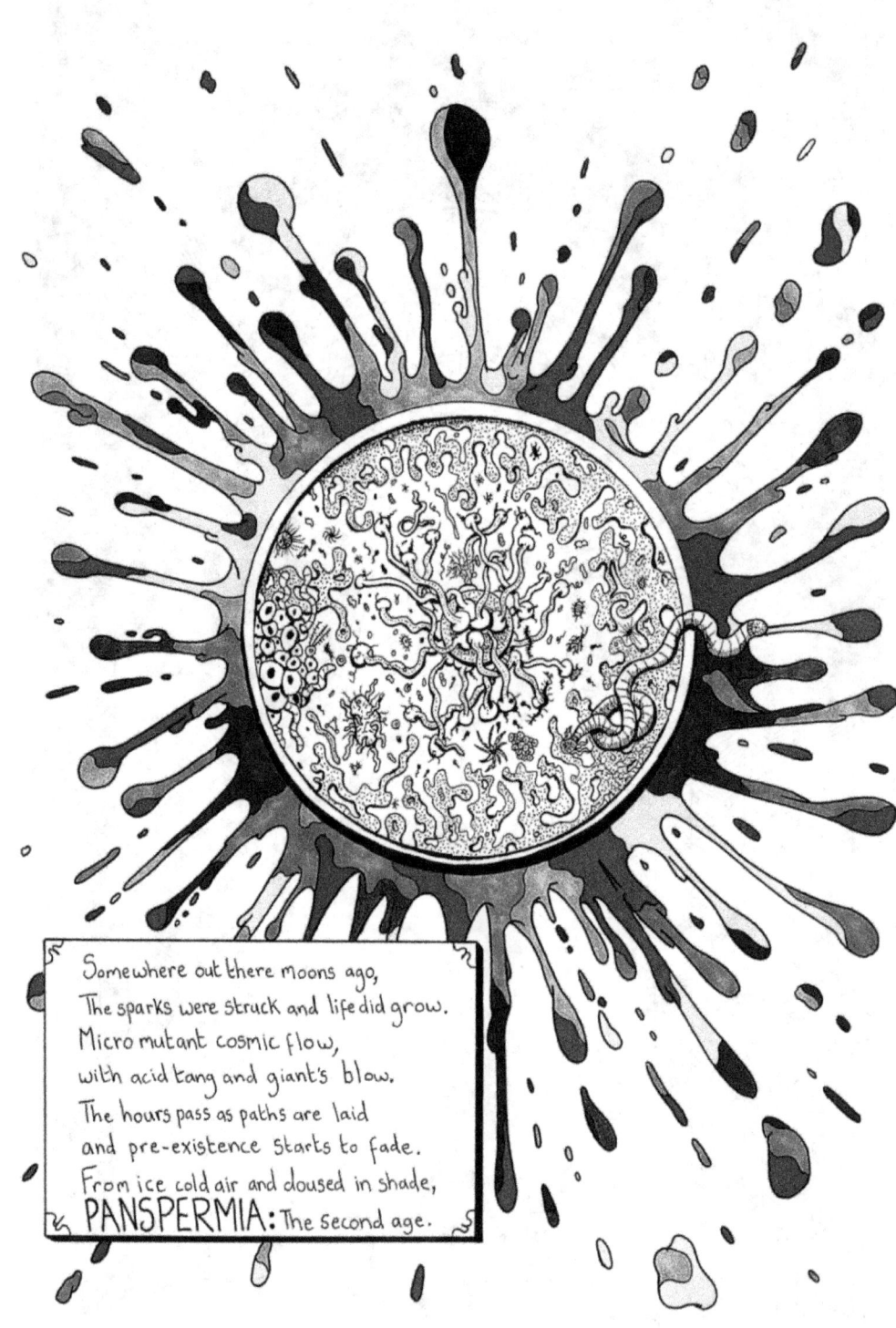

Somewhere out there moons ago,
The sparks were struck and life did grow.
Micro mutant cosmic flow,
with acid tang and giant's blow.
The hours pass as paths are laid
and pre-existence starts to fade.
From ice cold air and doused in shade,
PANSPERMIA: The second age.

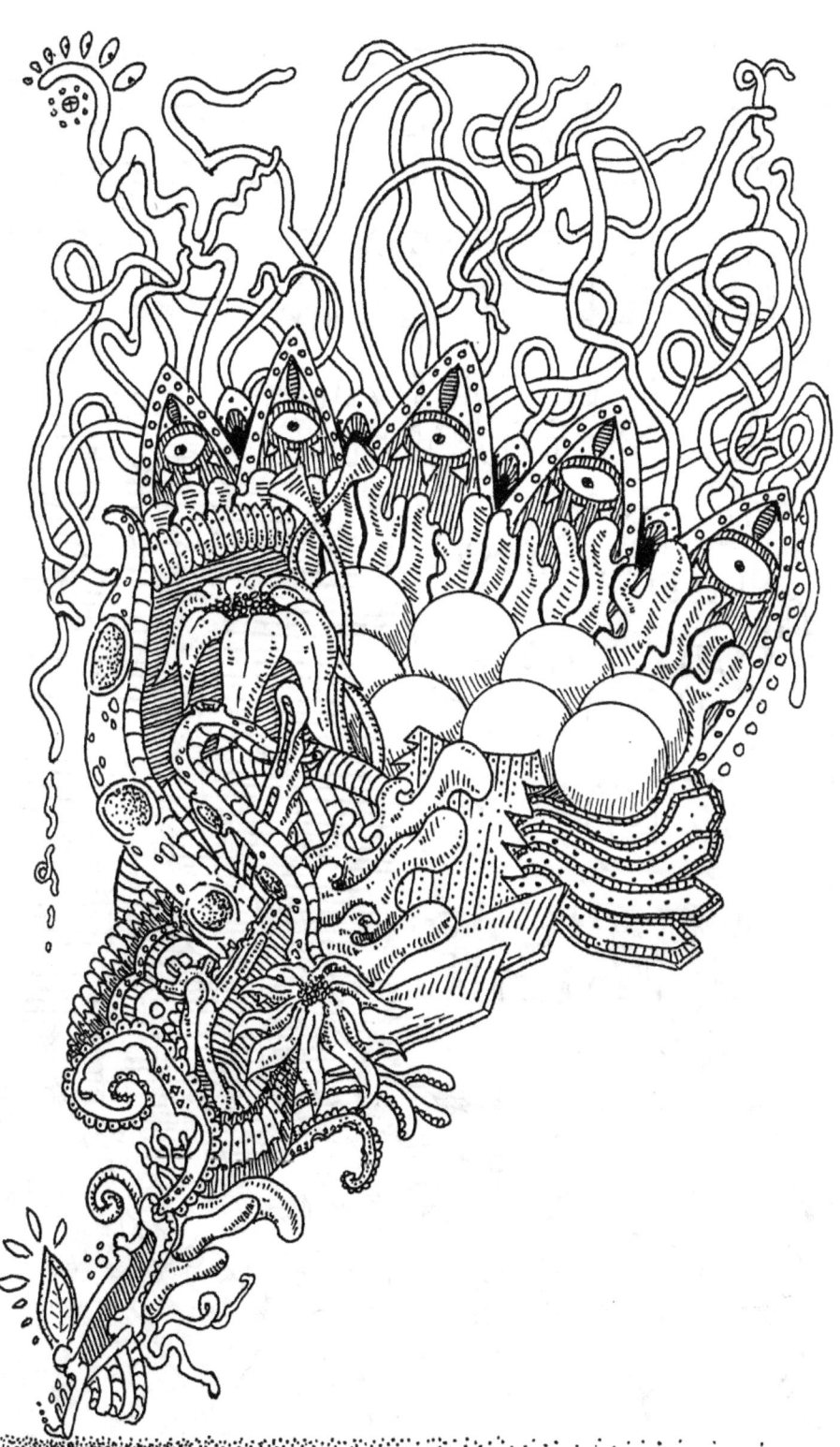

THE KEEPER of DREAMS HAS MUCH TO KEEP

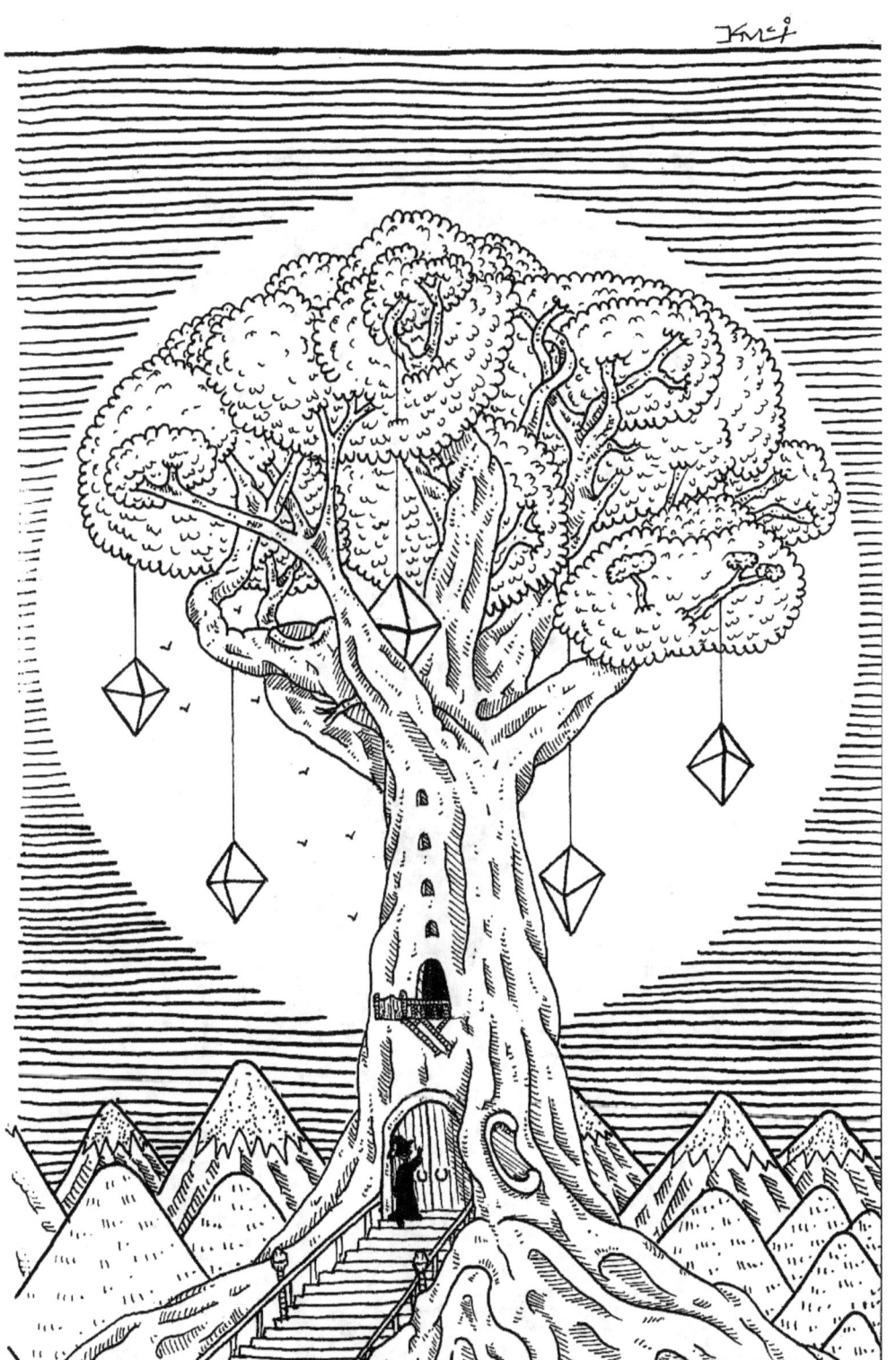

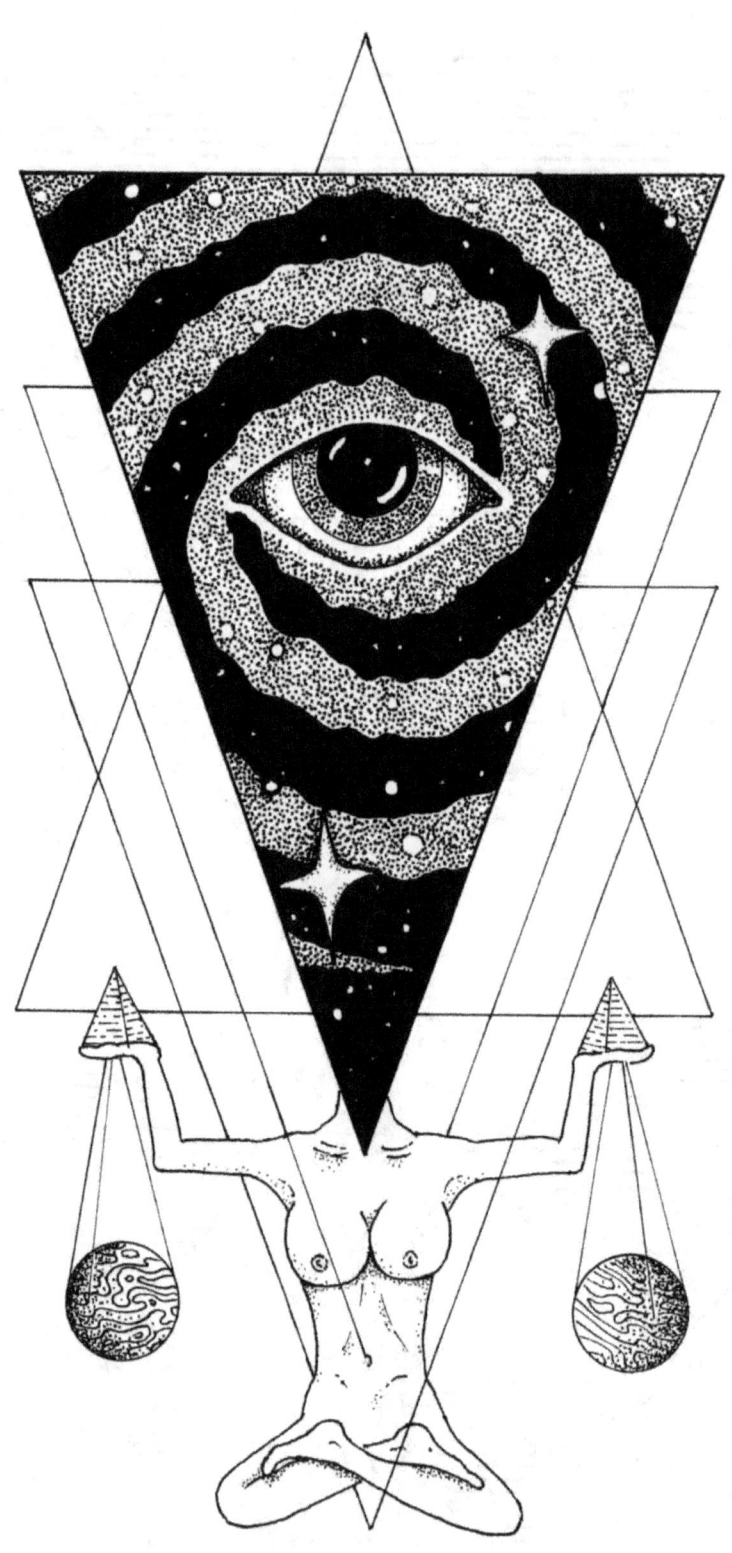

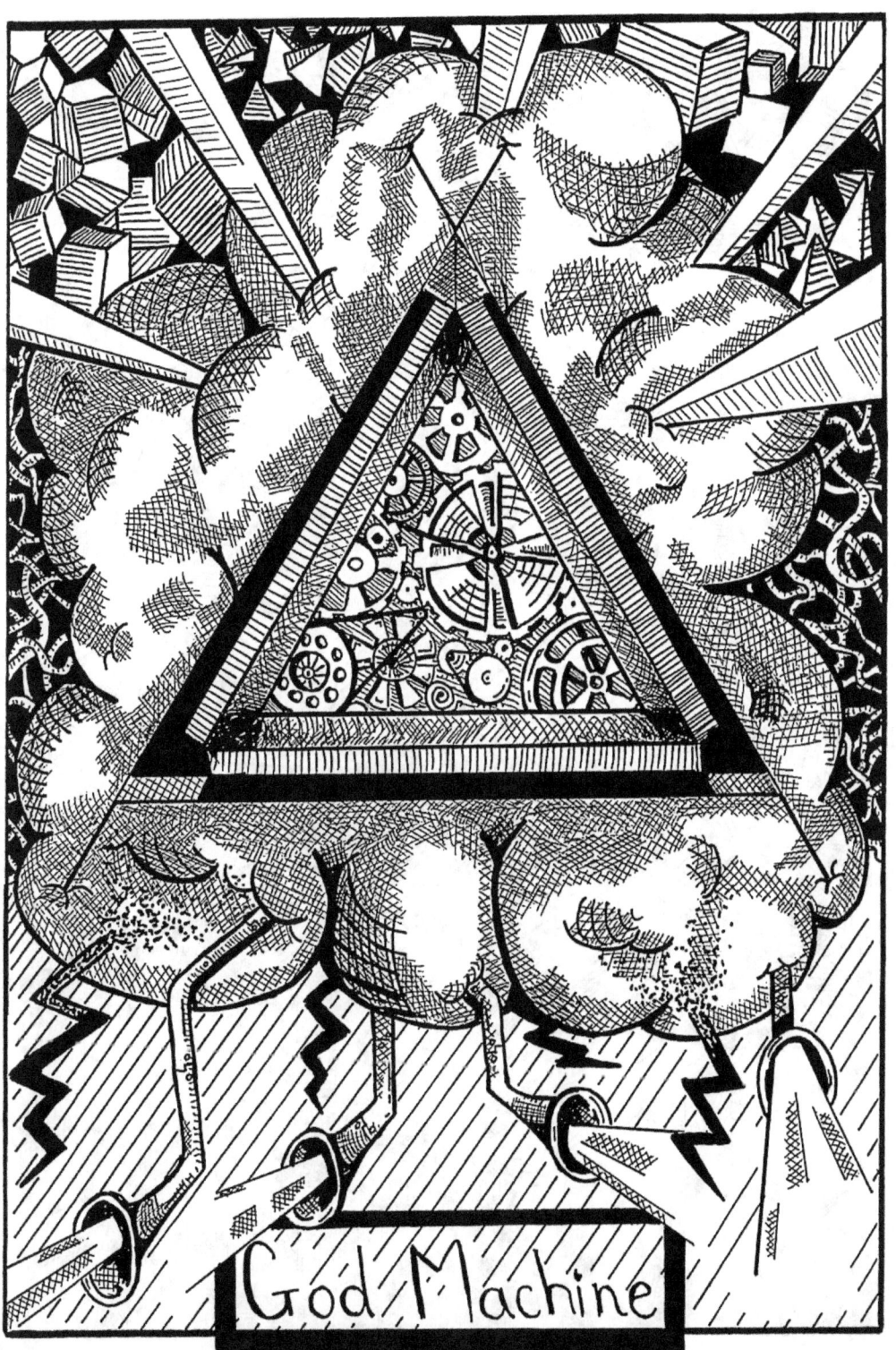

God Machine

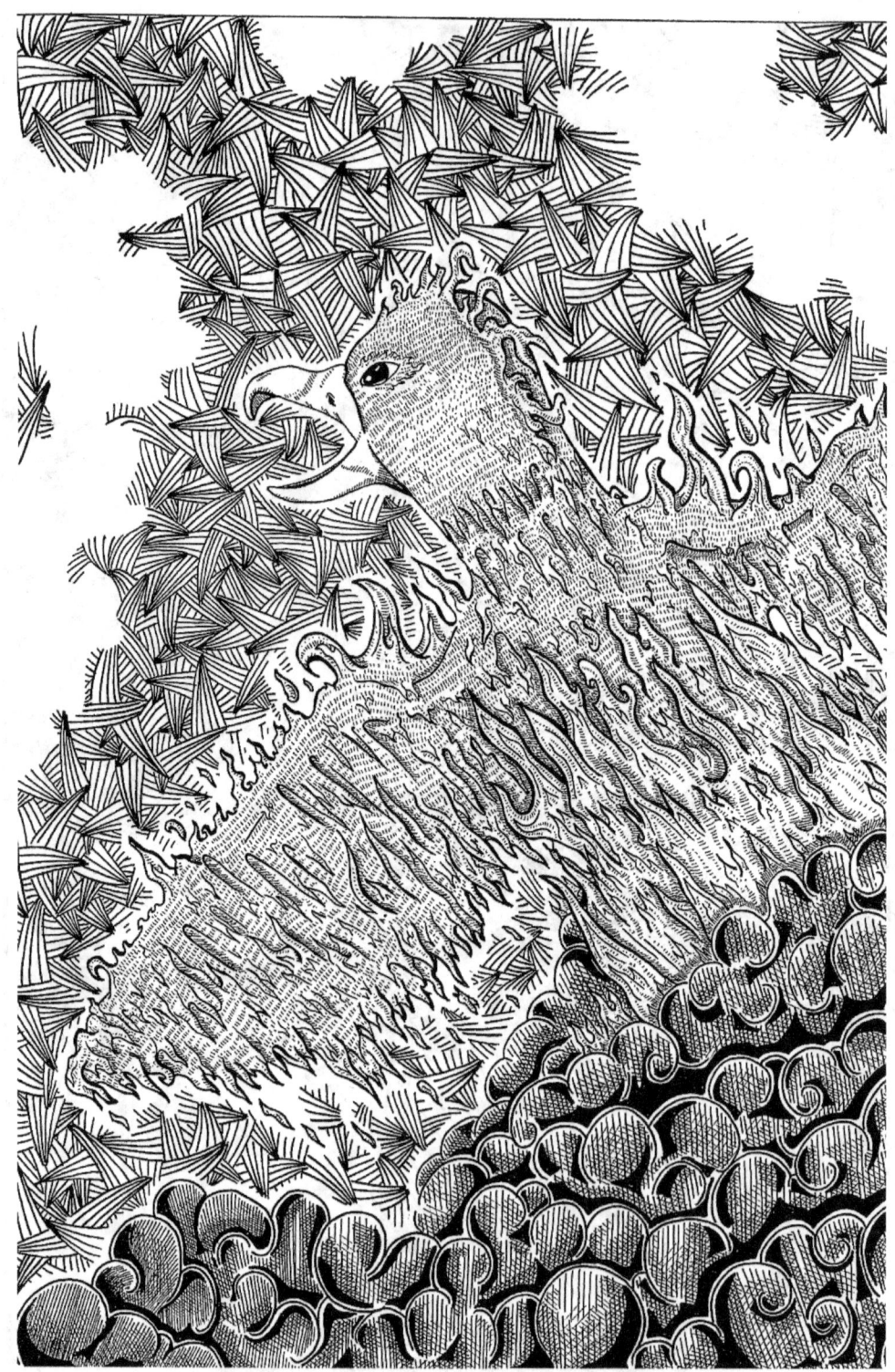

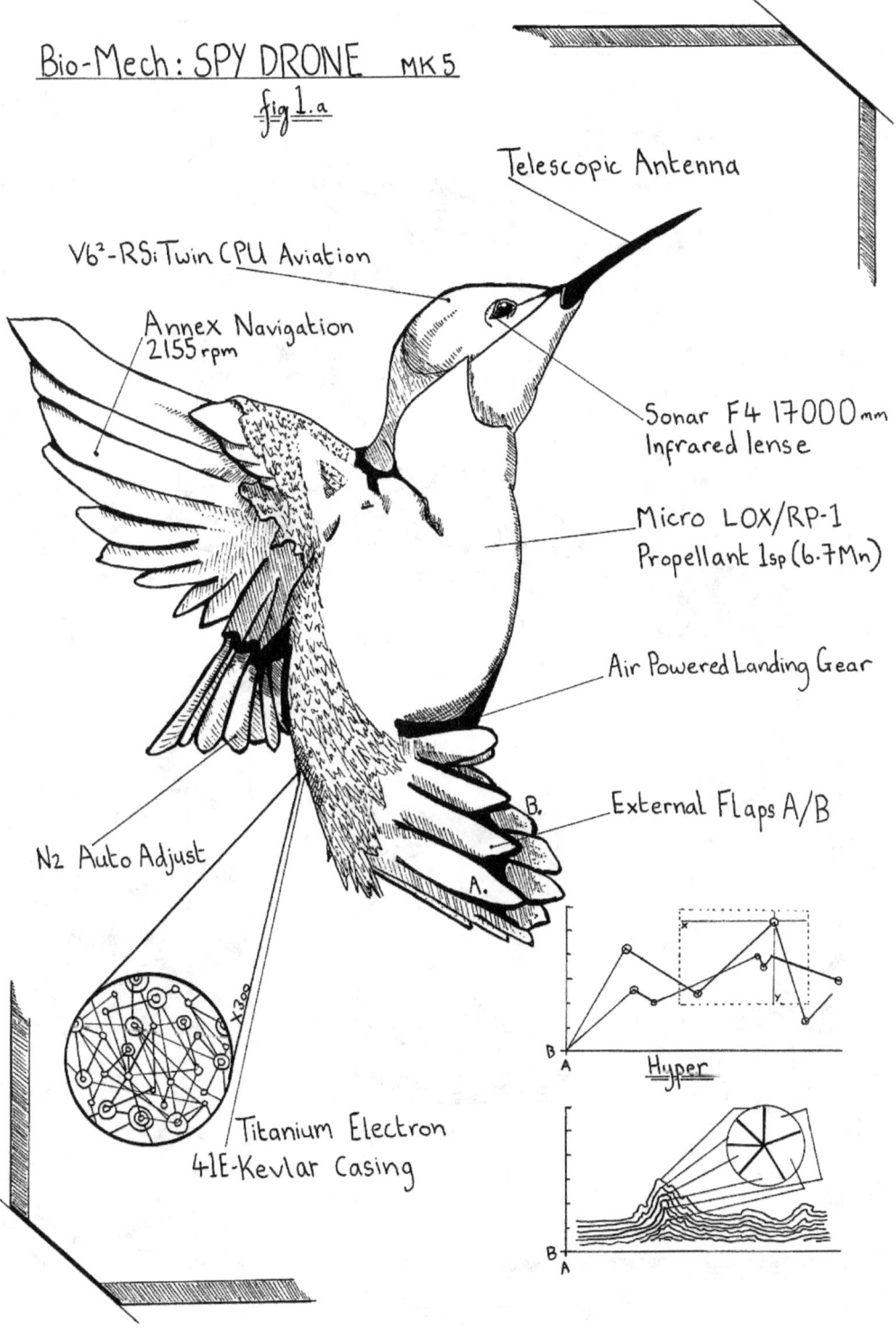

Bio-Mech: SPY DRONE MK5
fig 1.a

Telescopic Antenna

V6²-RSi Twin CPU Aviation

Annex Navigation
2155 rpm

Sonar F4 17000 mm
Infrared lense

Micro LOX/RP-1
Propellant Isp (6.7 Mn)

Air Powered Landing Gear

External Flaps A/B

B.

A.

N2 Auto Adjust

X39

Titanium Electron
41E-Kevlar Casing

B
A
Hyper

B
A

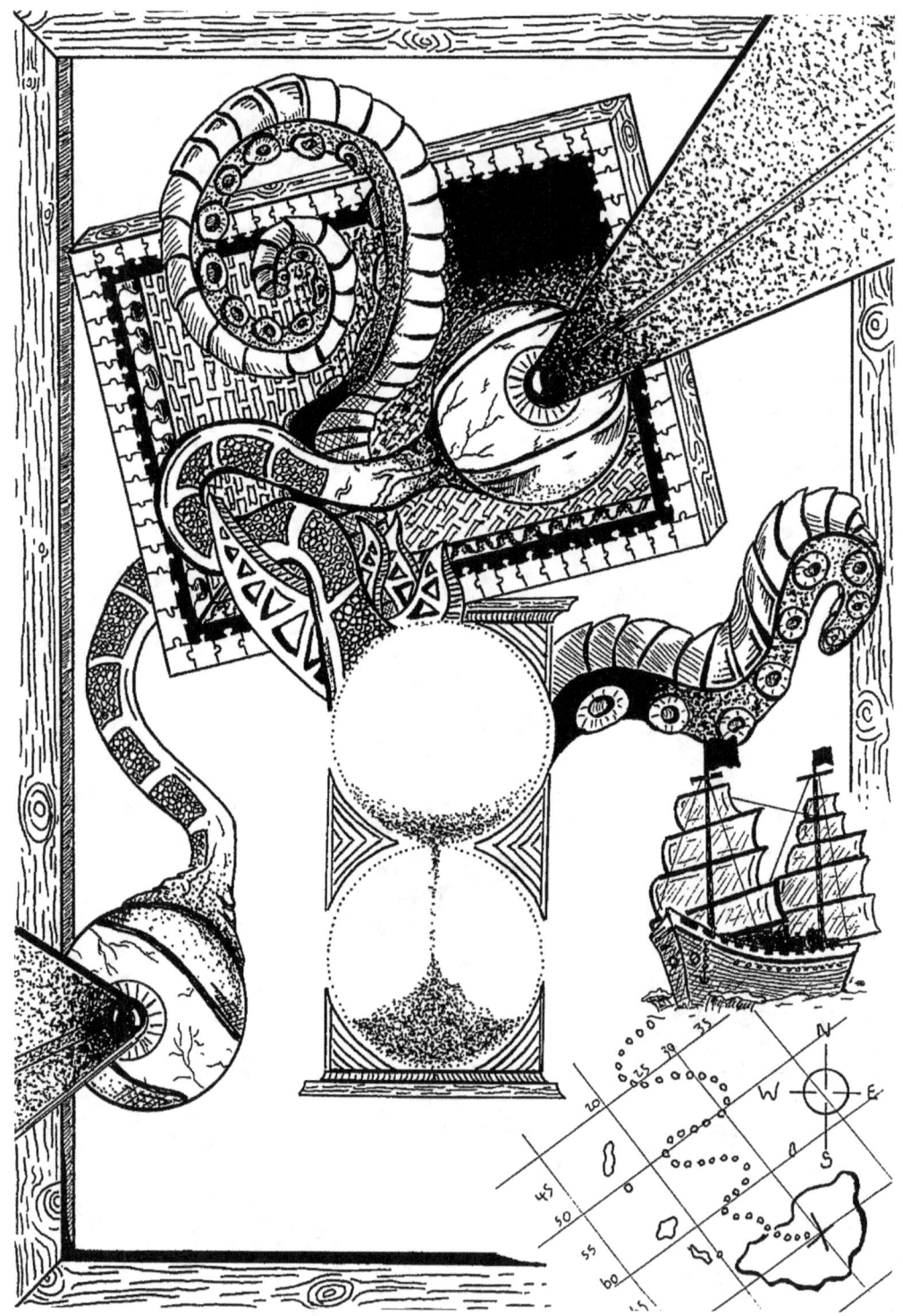

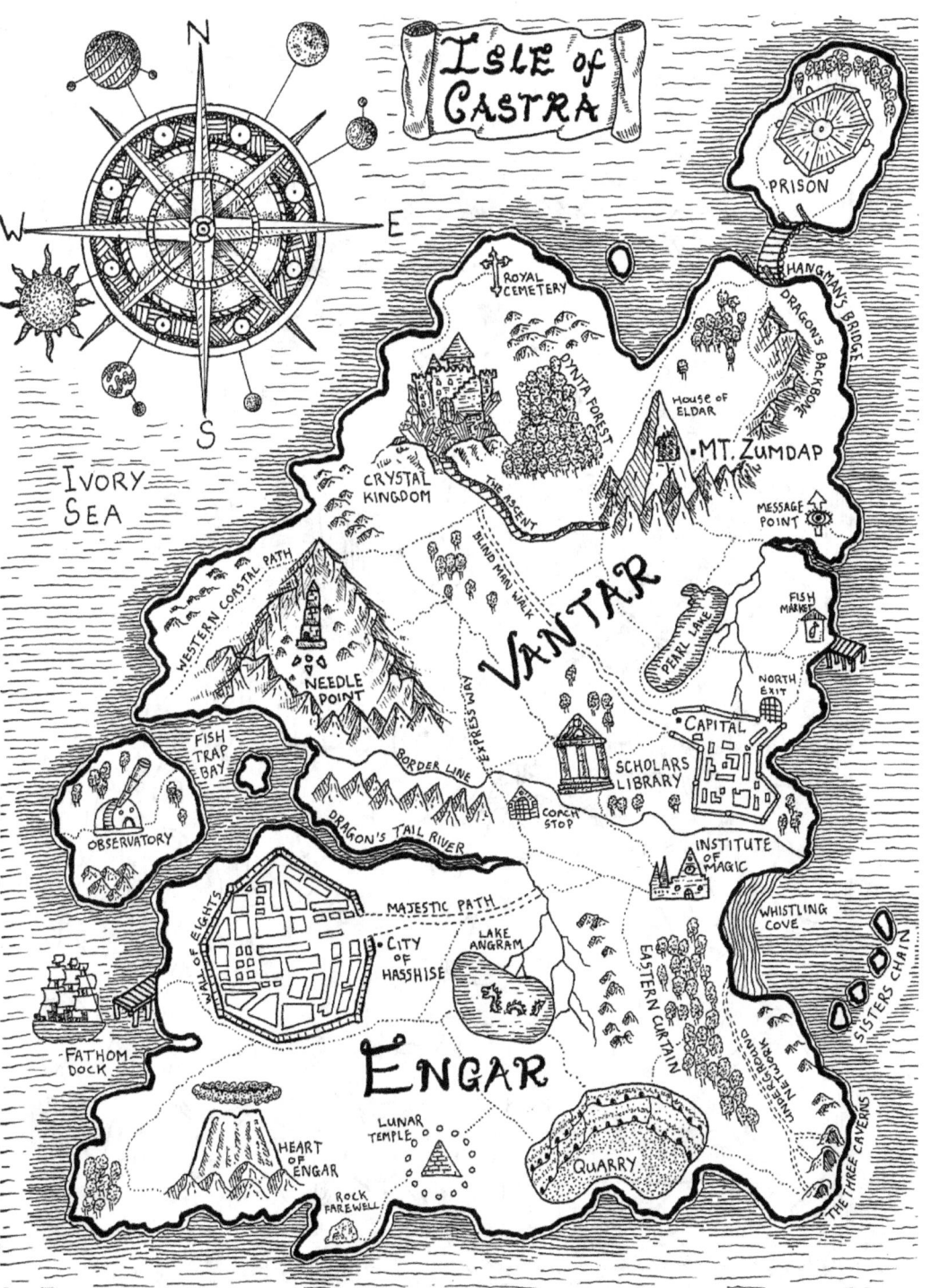

ORIFICE

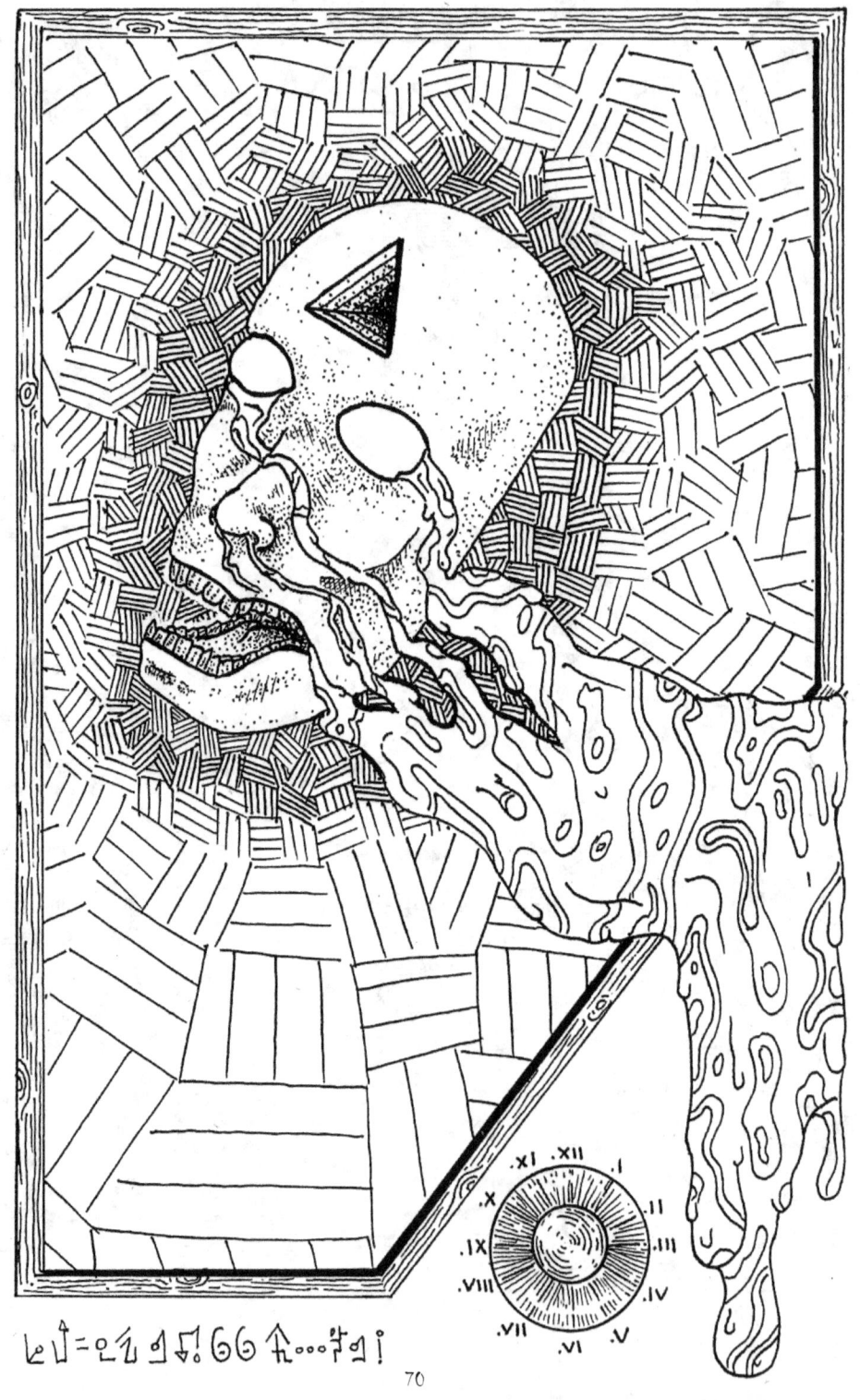

70

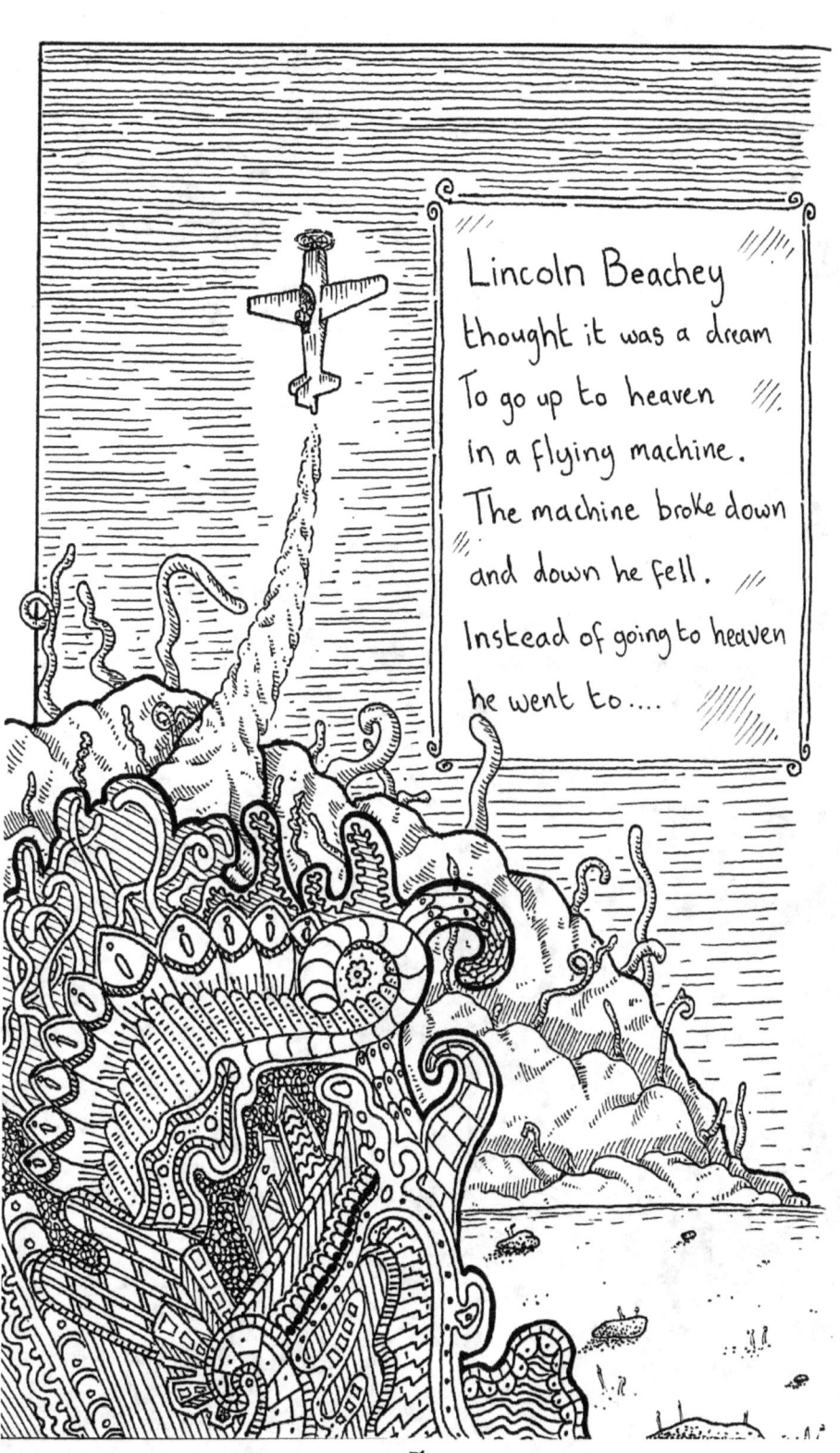

Lincoln Beachey
thought it was a dream
To go up to heaven
in a flying machine.
The machine broke down
and down he fell.
Instead of going to heaven
he went to....

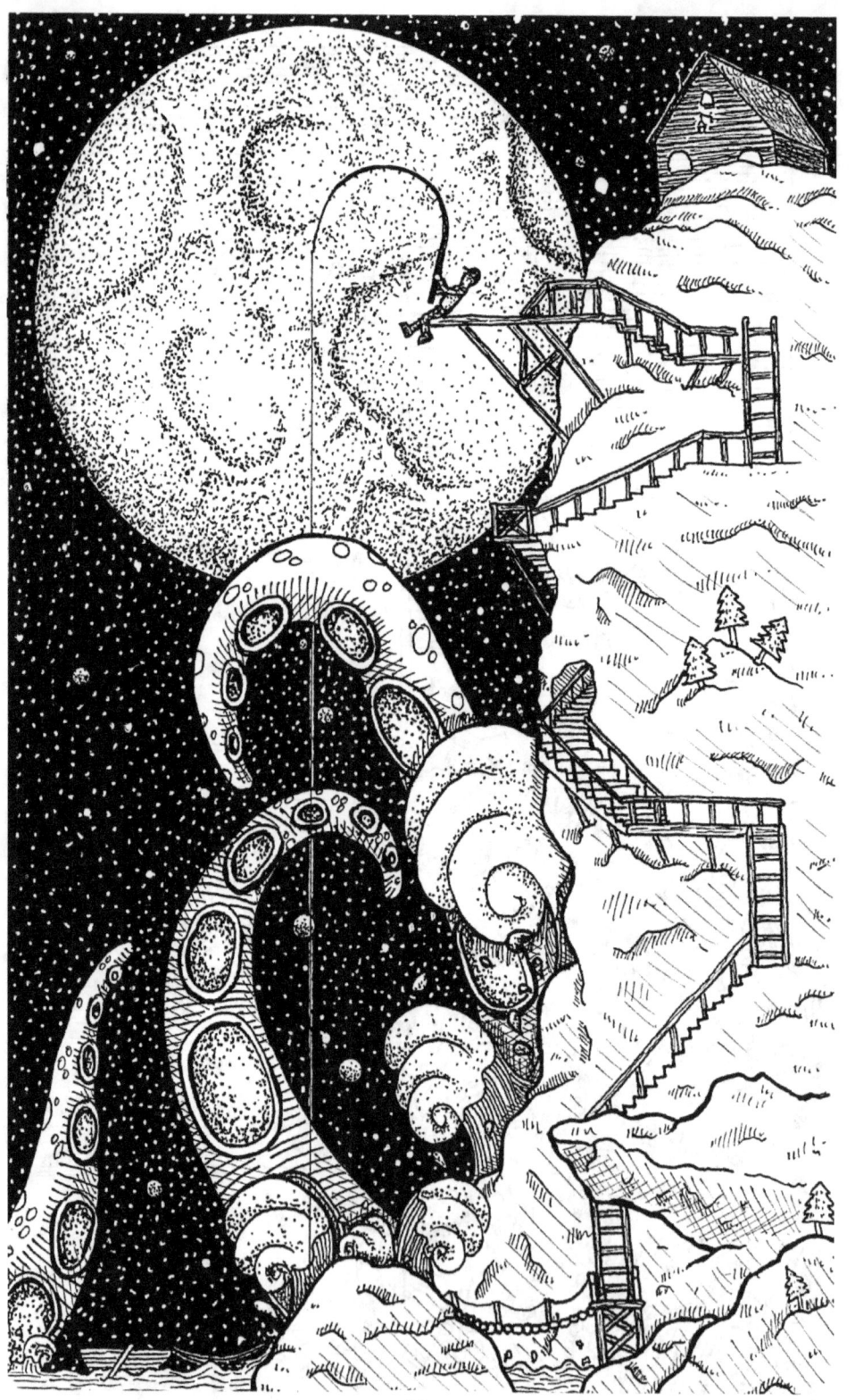

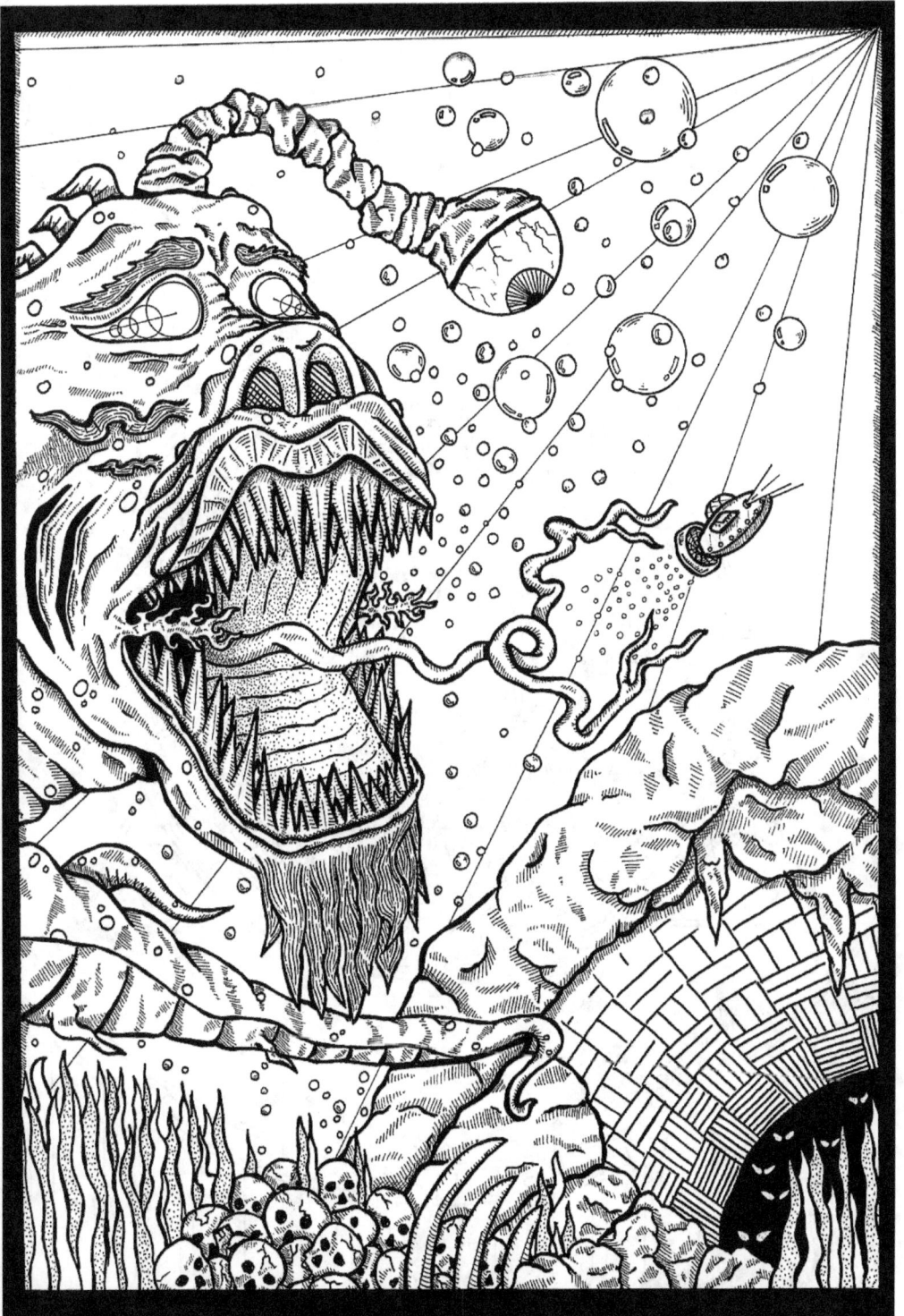

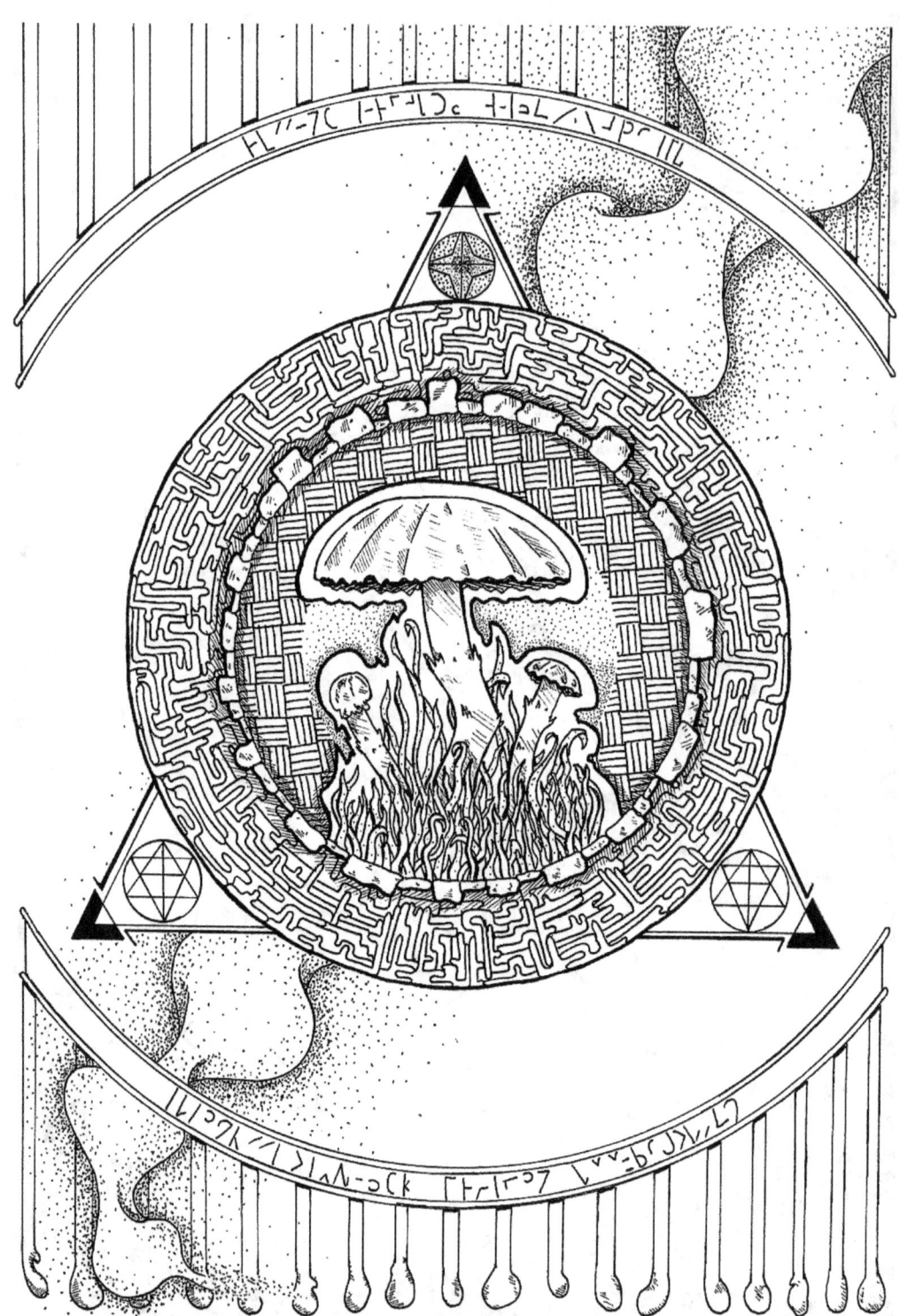

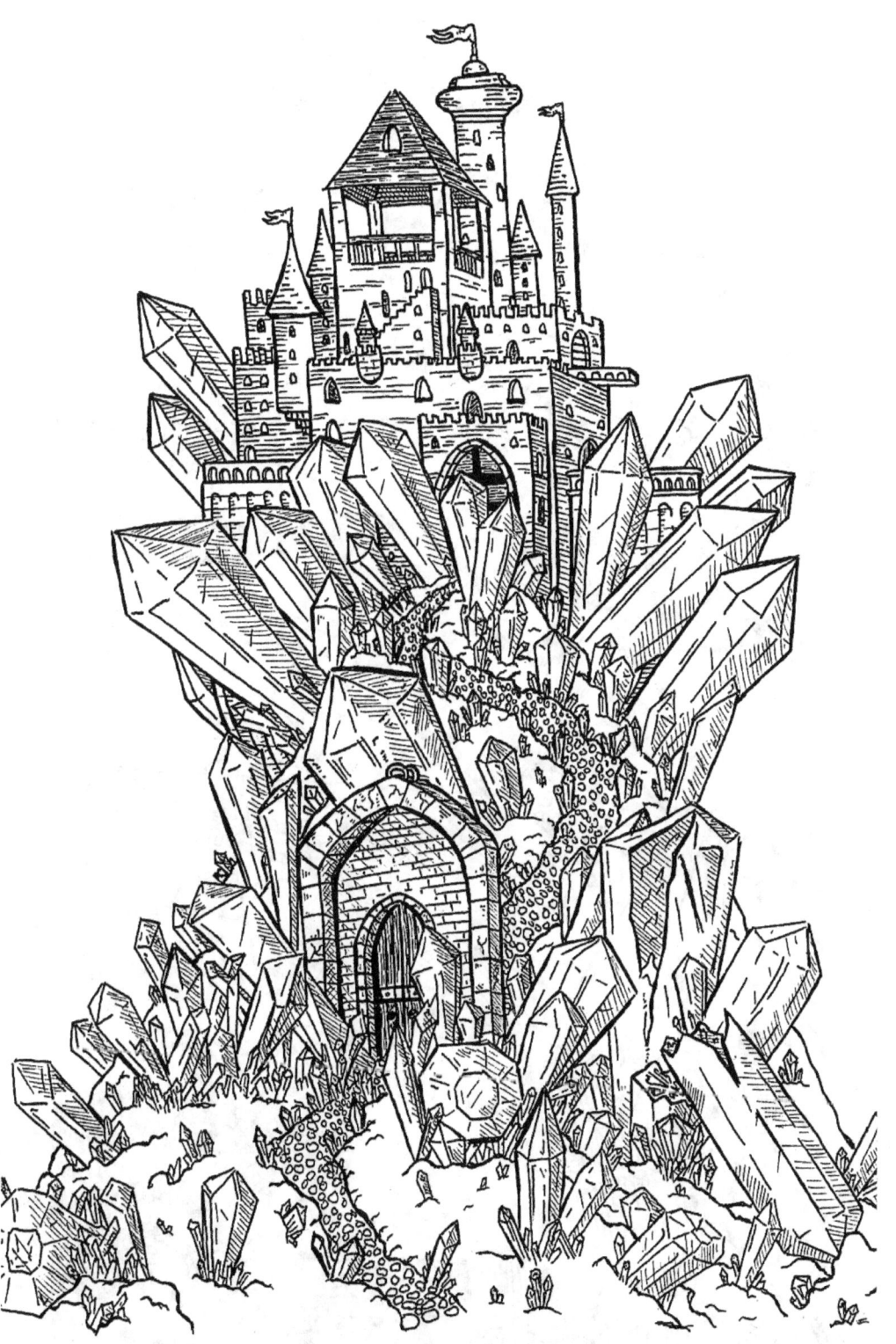

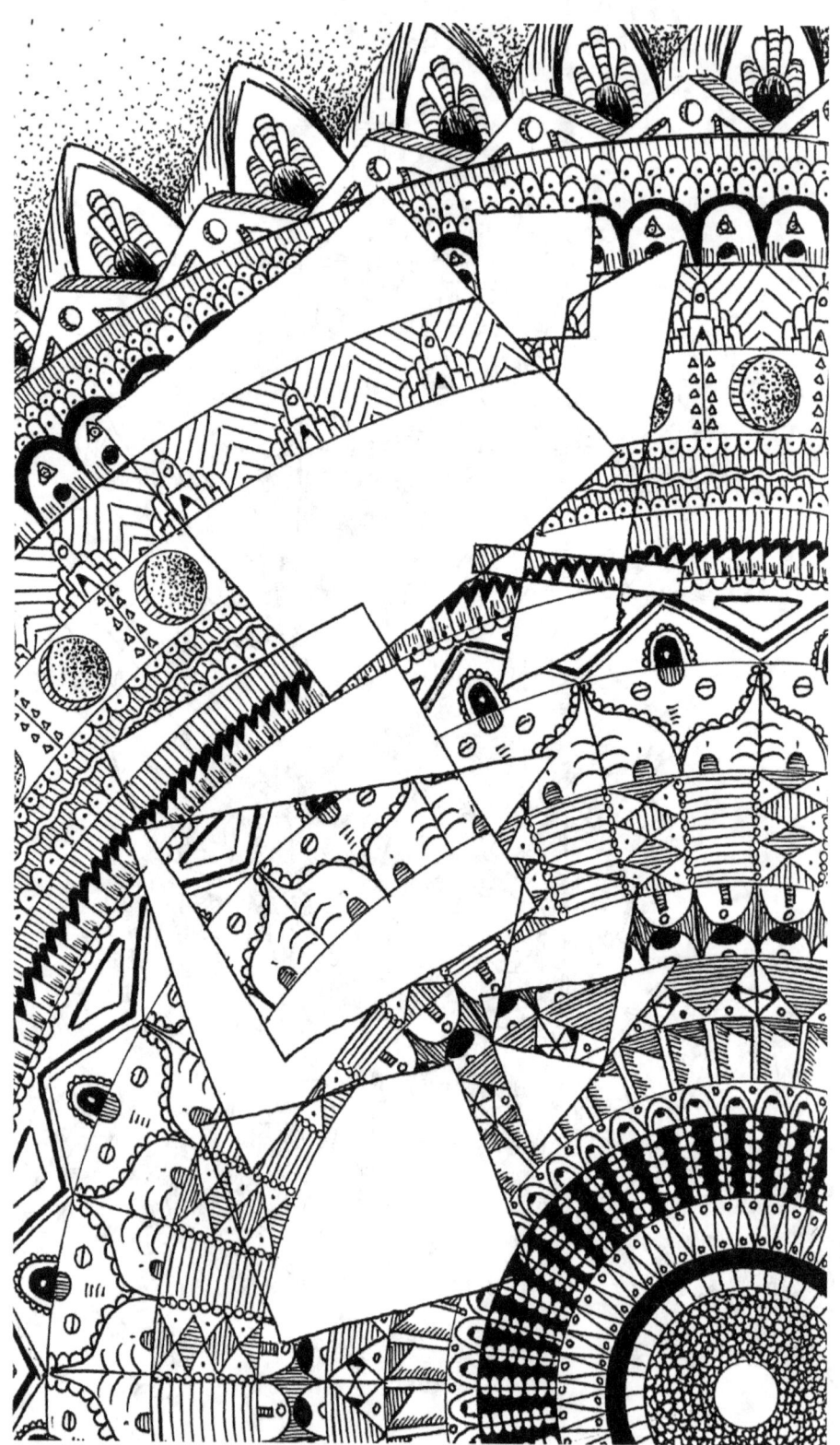

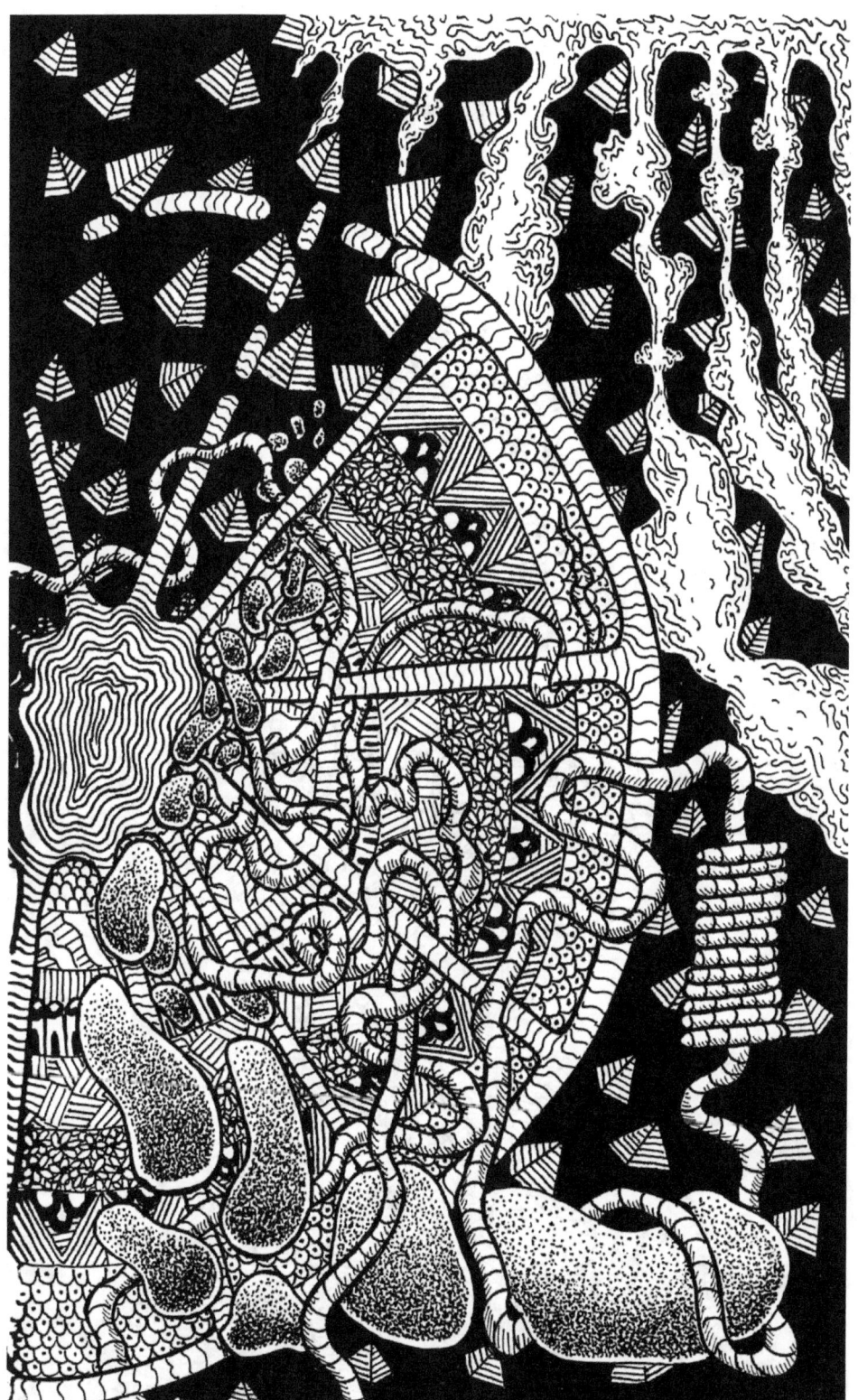

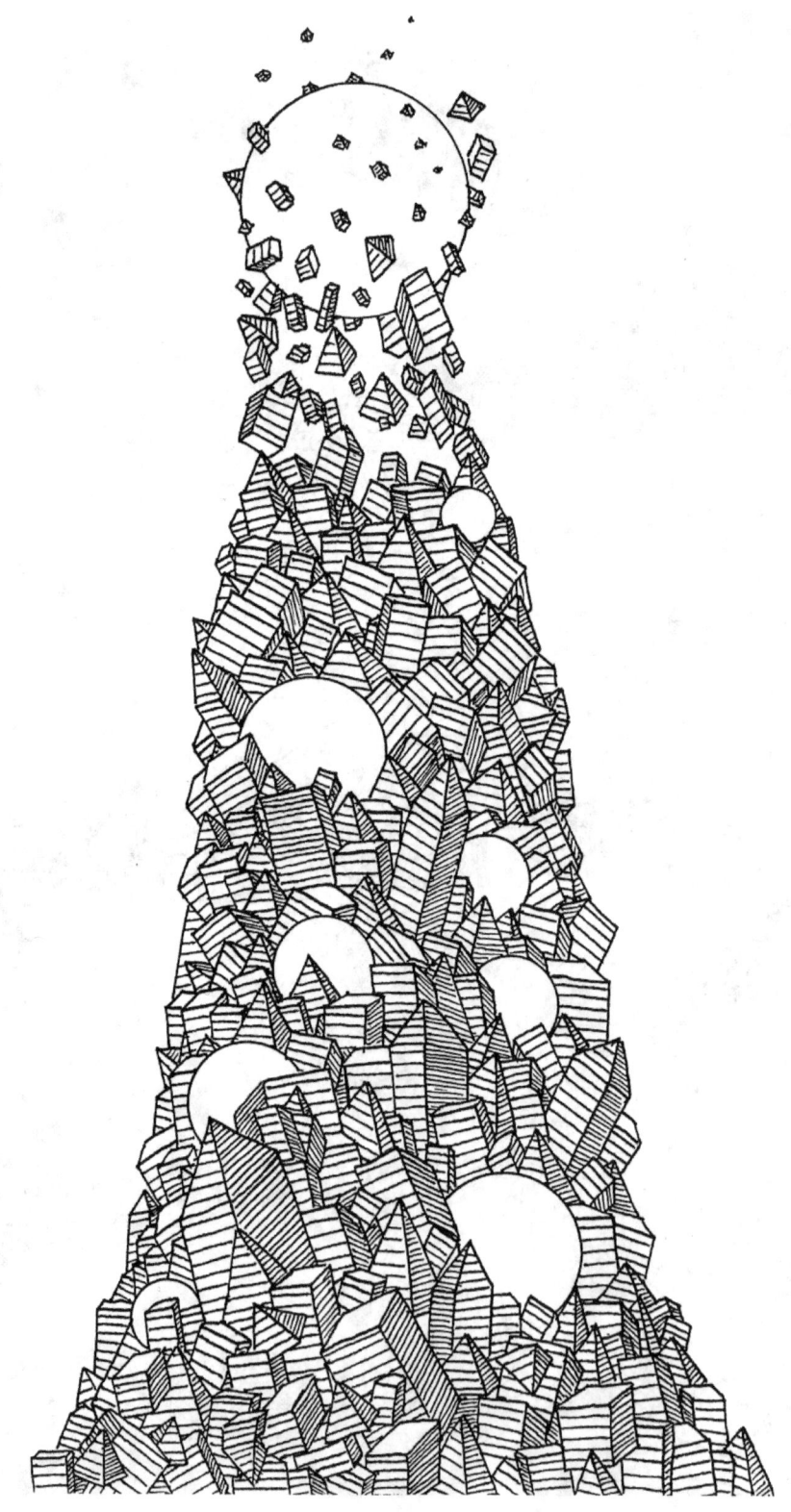

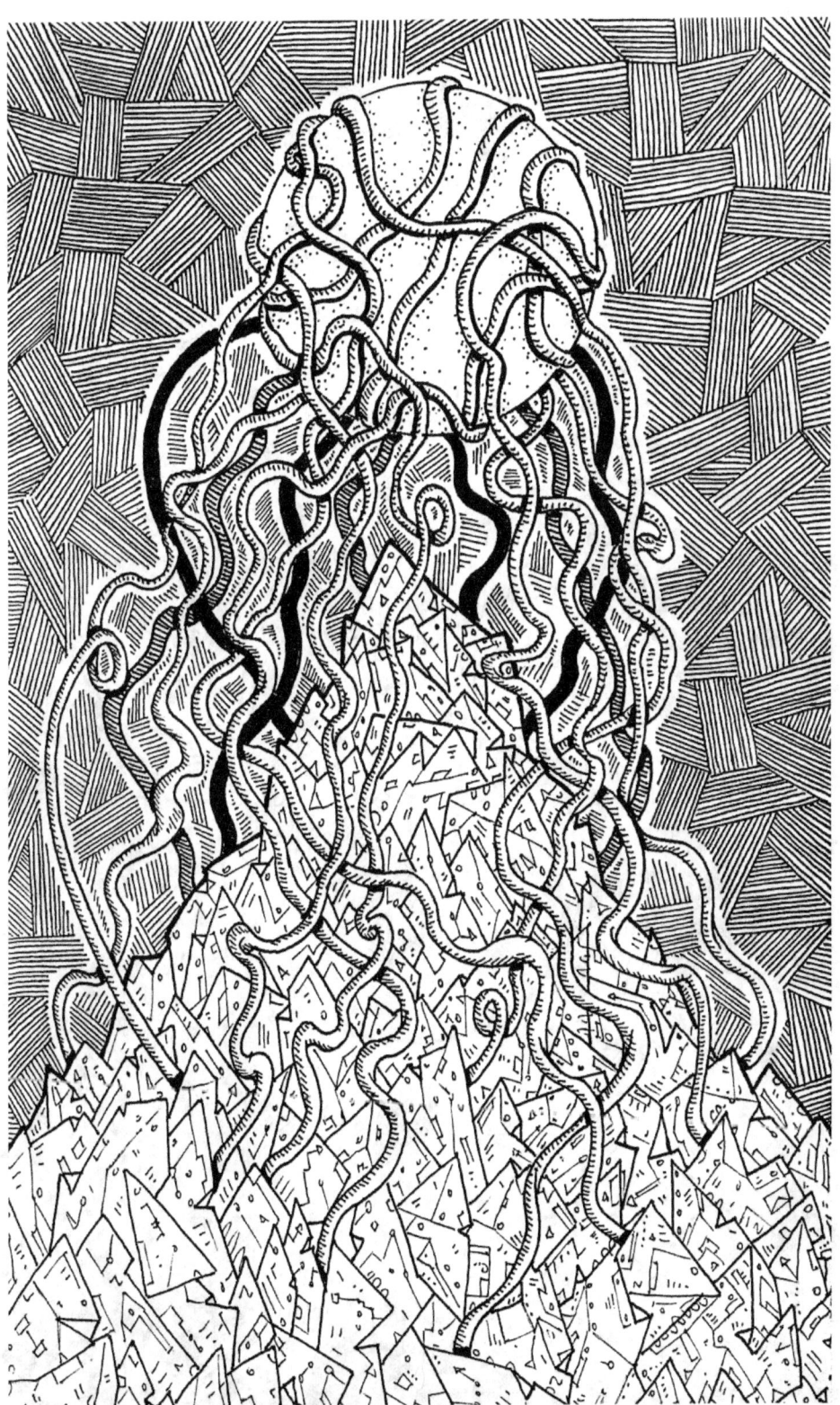

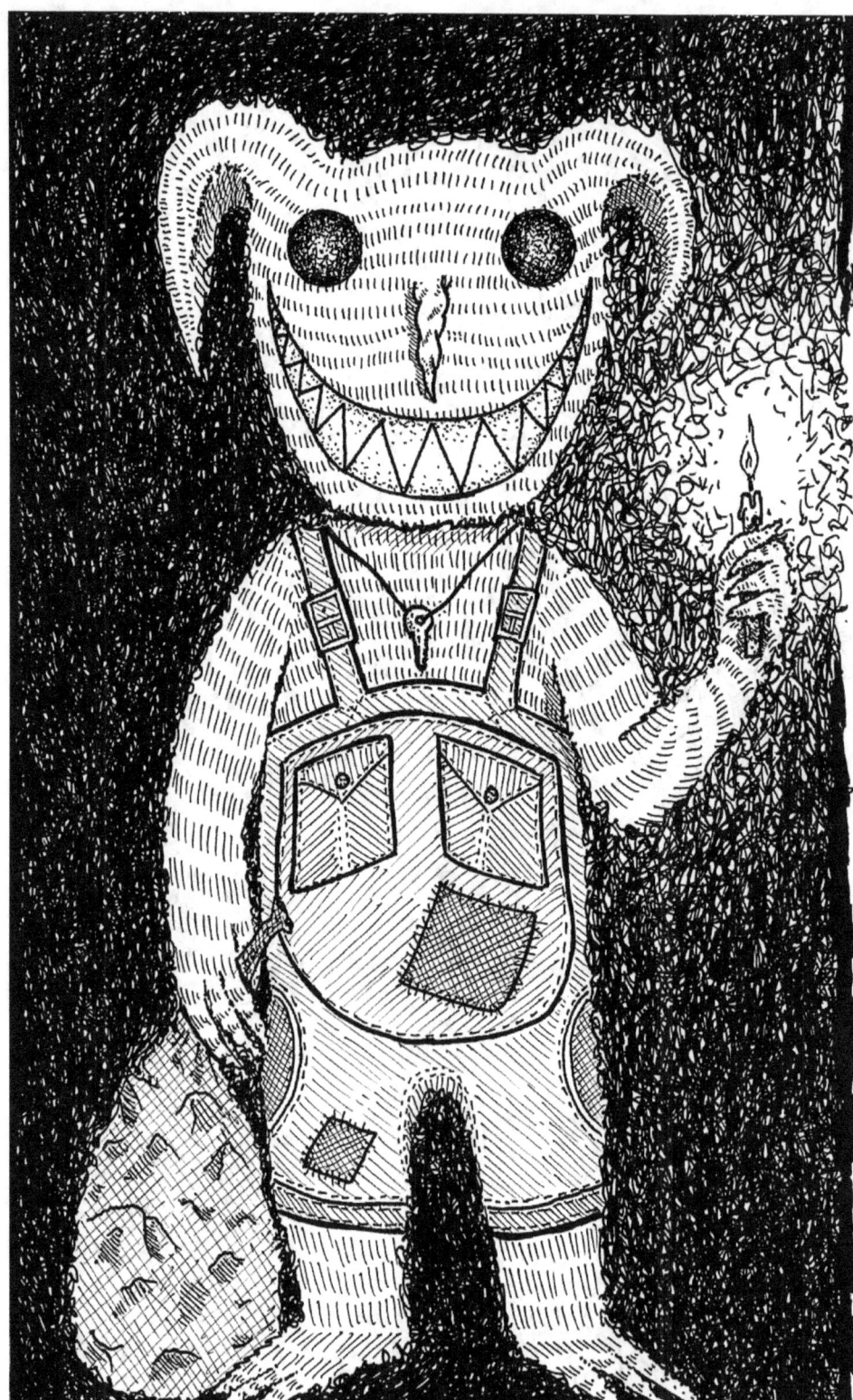

What is it that guides you in the deepest
Catacombs of your mind?

Is it fear, jealousy and anger, plus a
Vocabulary drenched in hate?

I am all of these. I am all that there is.
All of your learned and predetermined
Vulgarities, marinated over and over and over
and

In my right hand. I carry a pulsating,
rotten sack of filth and dispair and I ache
for the moment to pick at the stitches
that bind it's neck.

In the other hand. I carry an ever dulling
candle. I trust in this to aid me in
choosing the correct paths ahead.

The light flickers as I make my choice.
I pause.....

A hideous smile from within beckons me
and I walk closer without hesitation.

Soon, I am now harbouring a deep grin.
My chapped lips pop and hiss as my face
dances from ear to ear.

Around my neck I wear the key.

The key to what?

That I do not know.
Although I do have an idea.

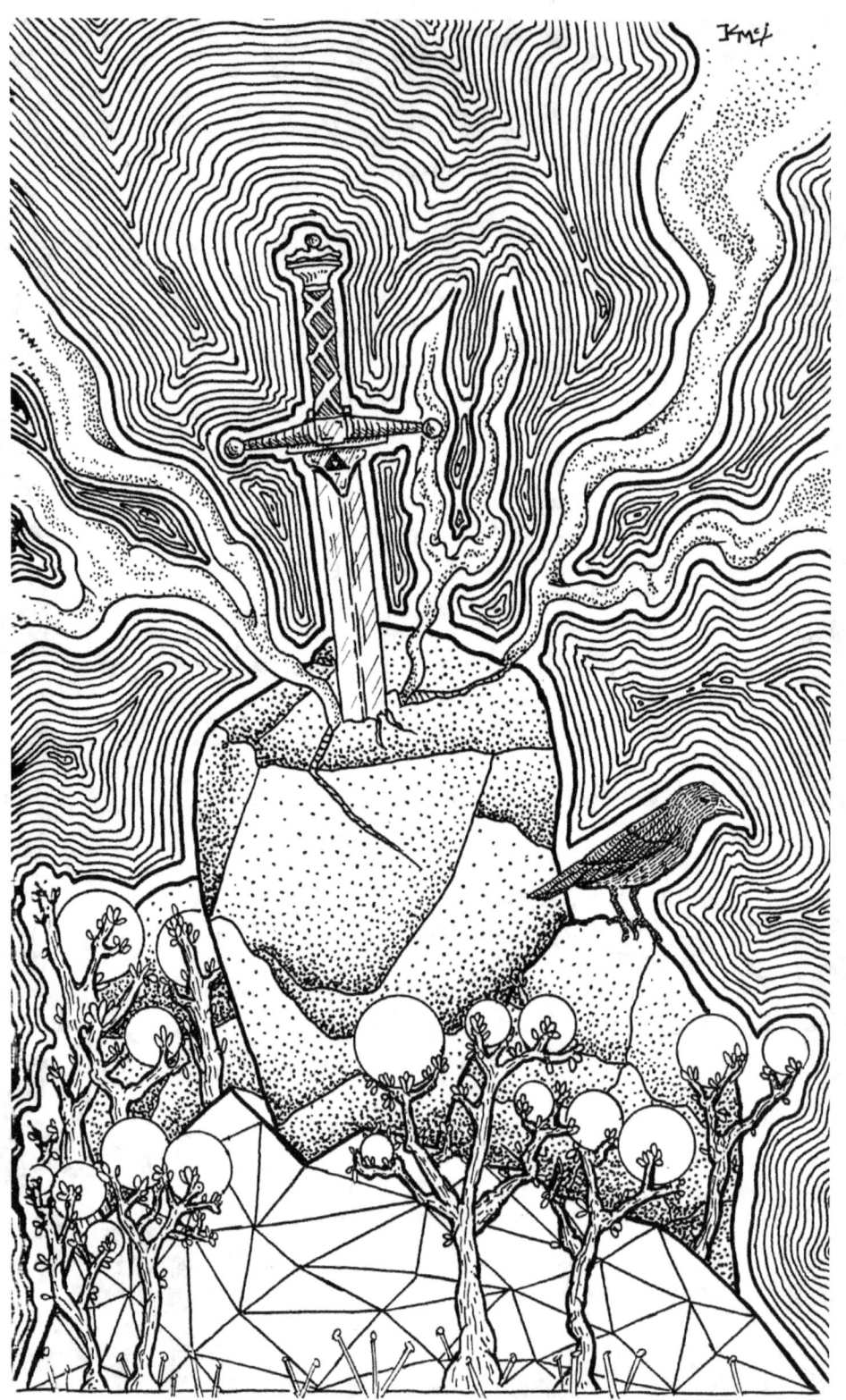

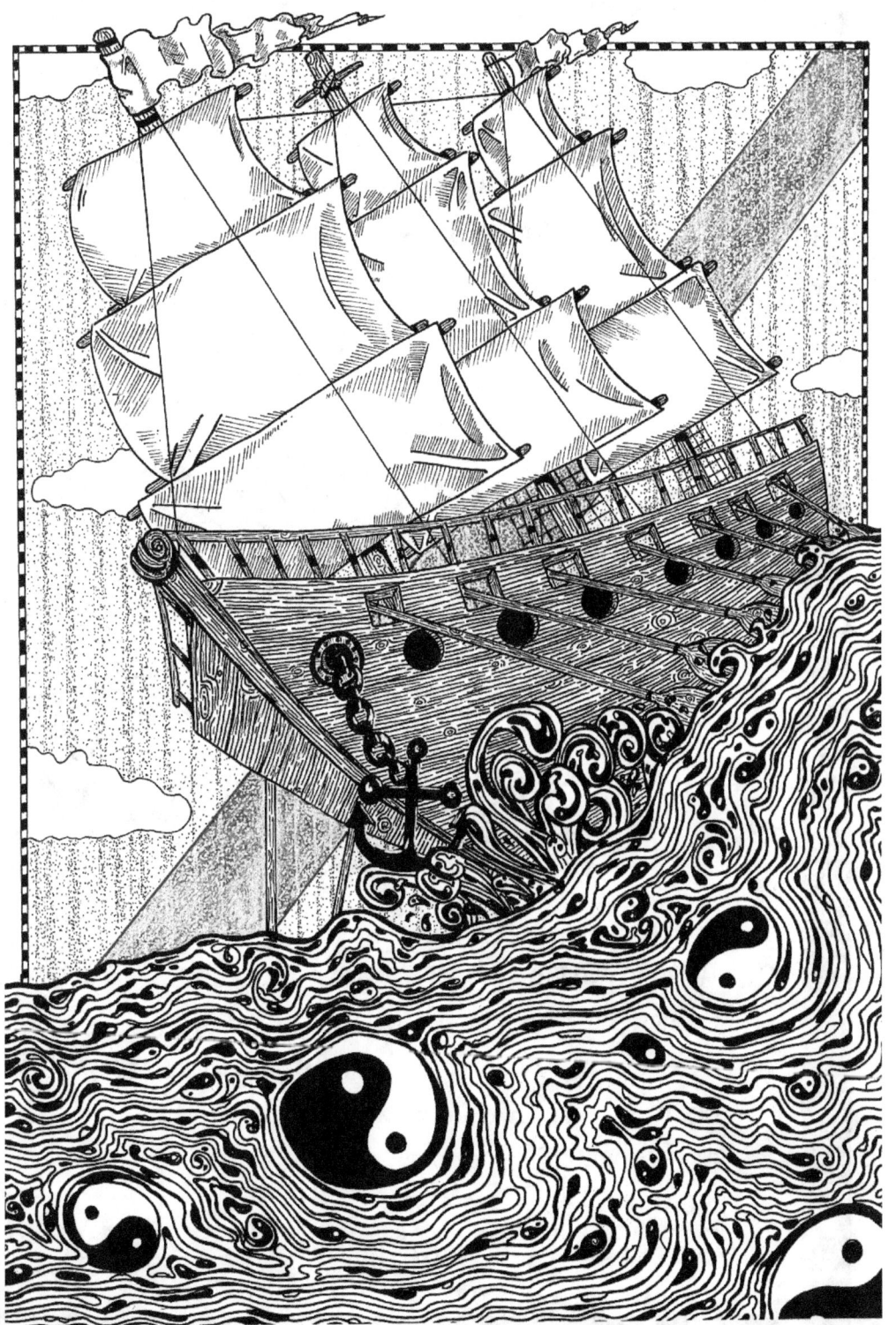

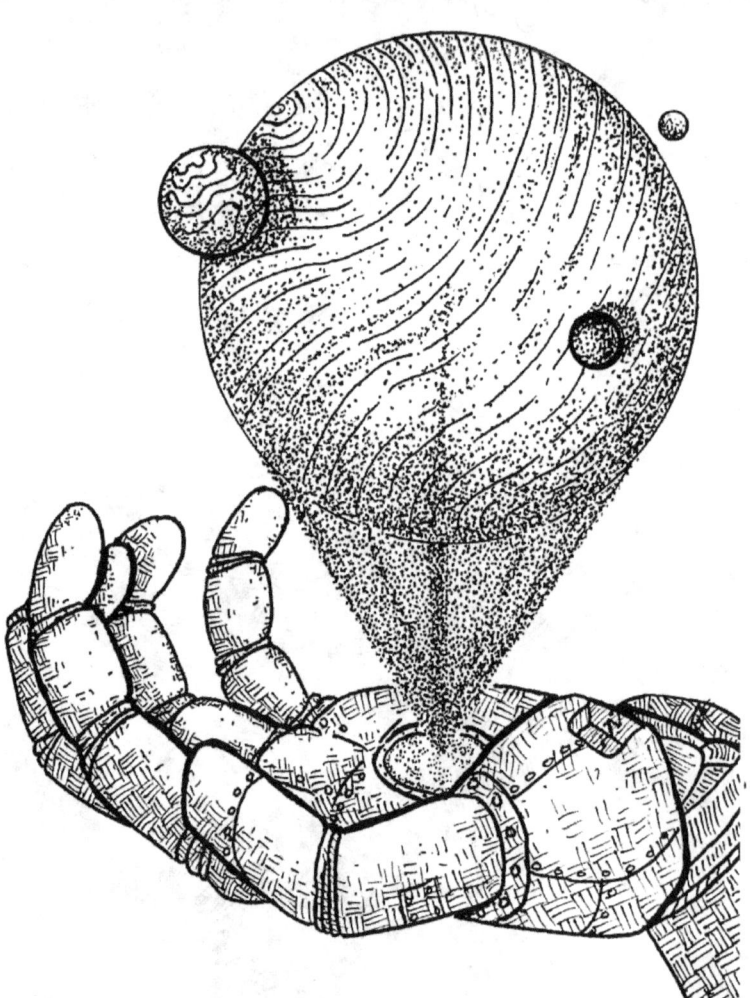

'If singularities exist at all it seems
easier to suppose that they might arise
out of an ancient and highly complexified
cosmos, such as our own, than out of
a featureless and dimensionless
mega-void.'
—Terence McKenna—

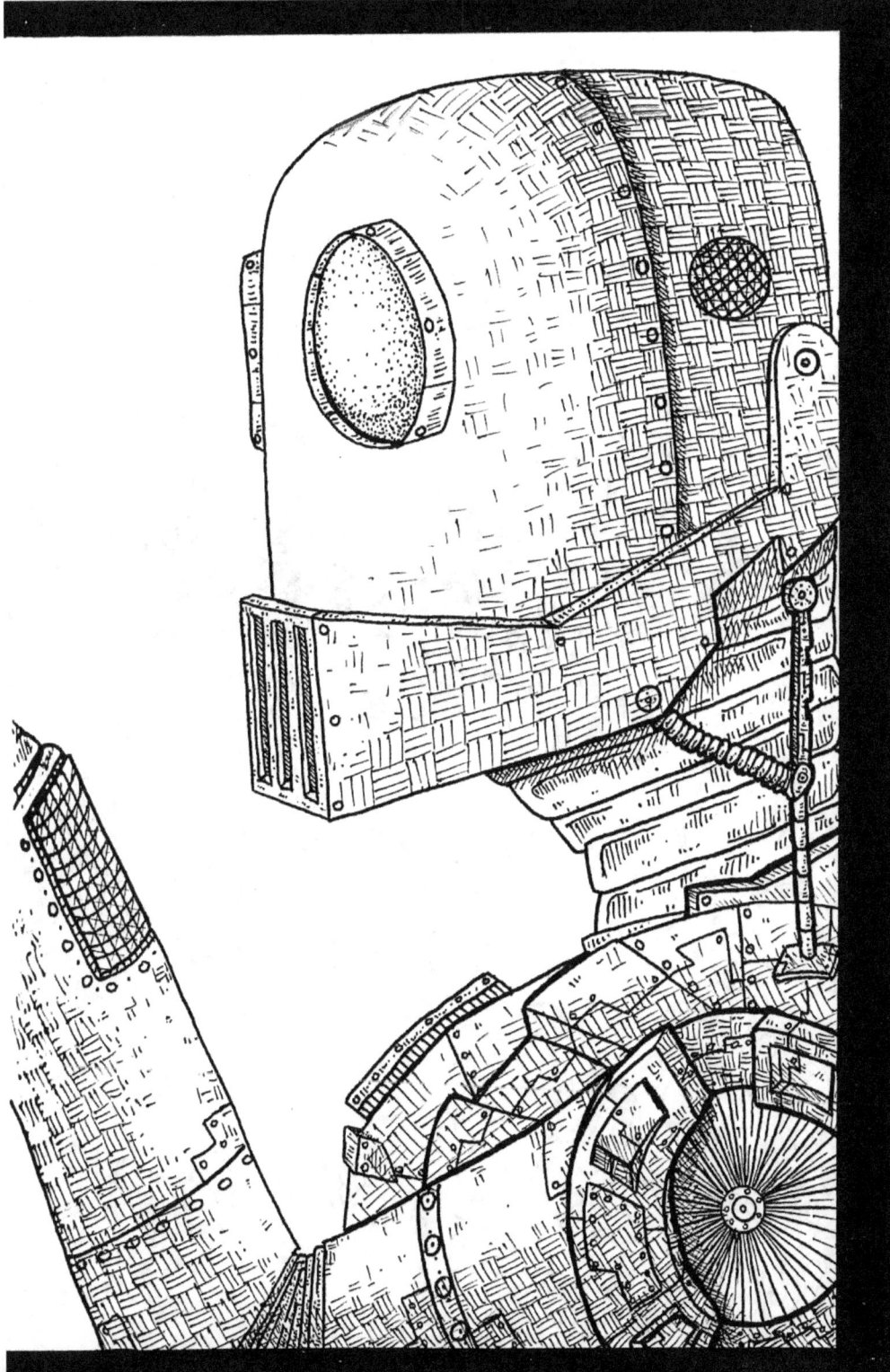

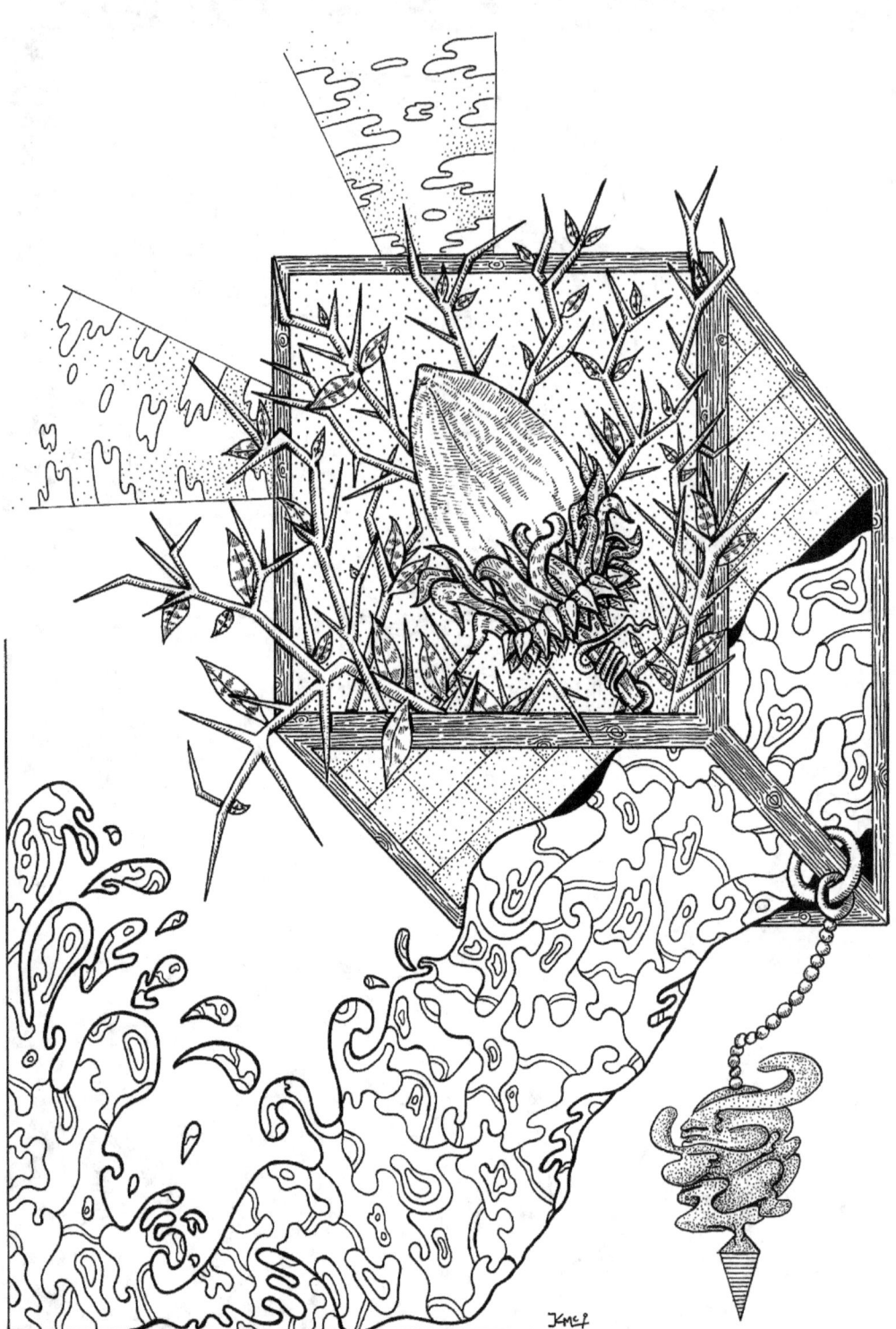

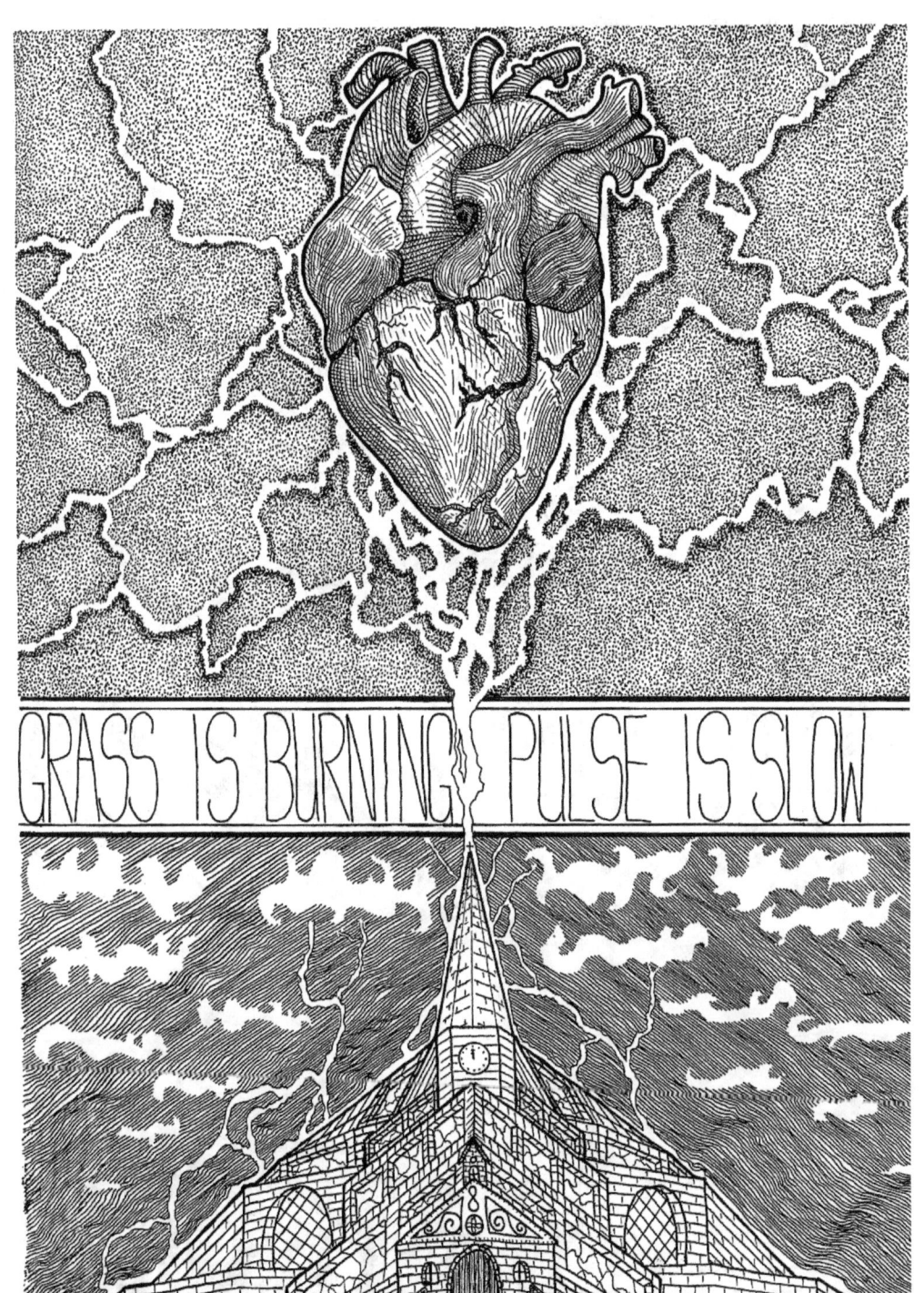

GRASS IS BURNING PULSE IS SLOW

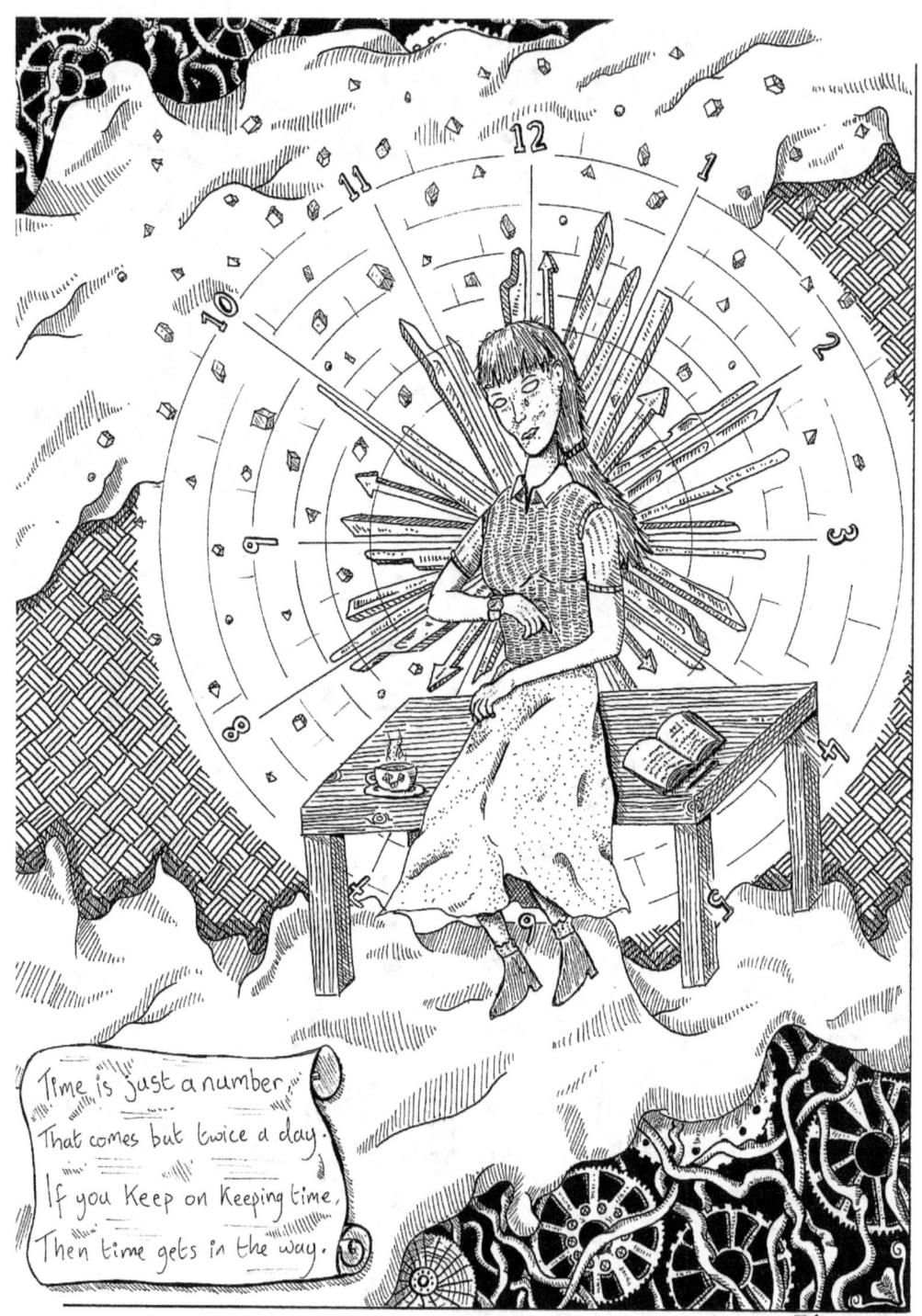

Time is just a number
That comes but twice a day.
If you Keep on Keeping time,
Then time gets in the way.

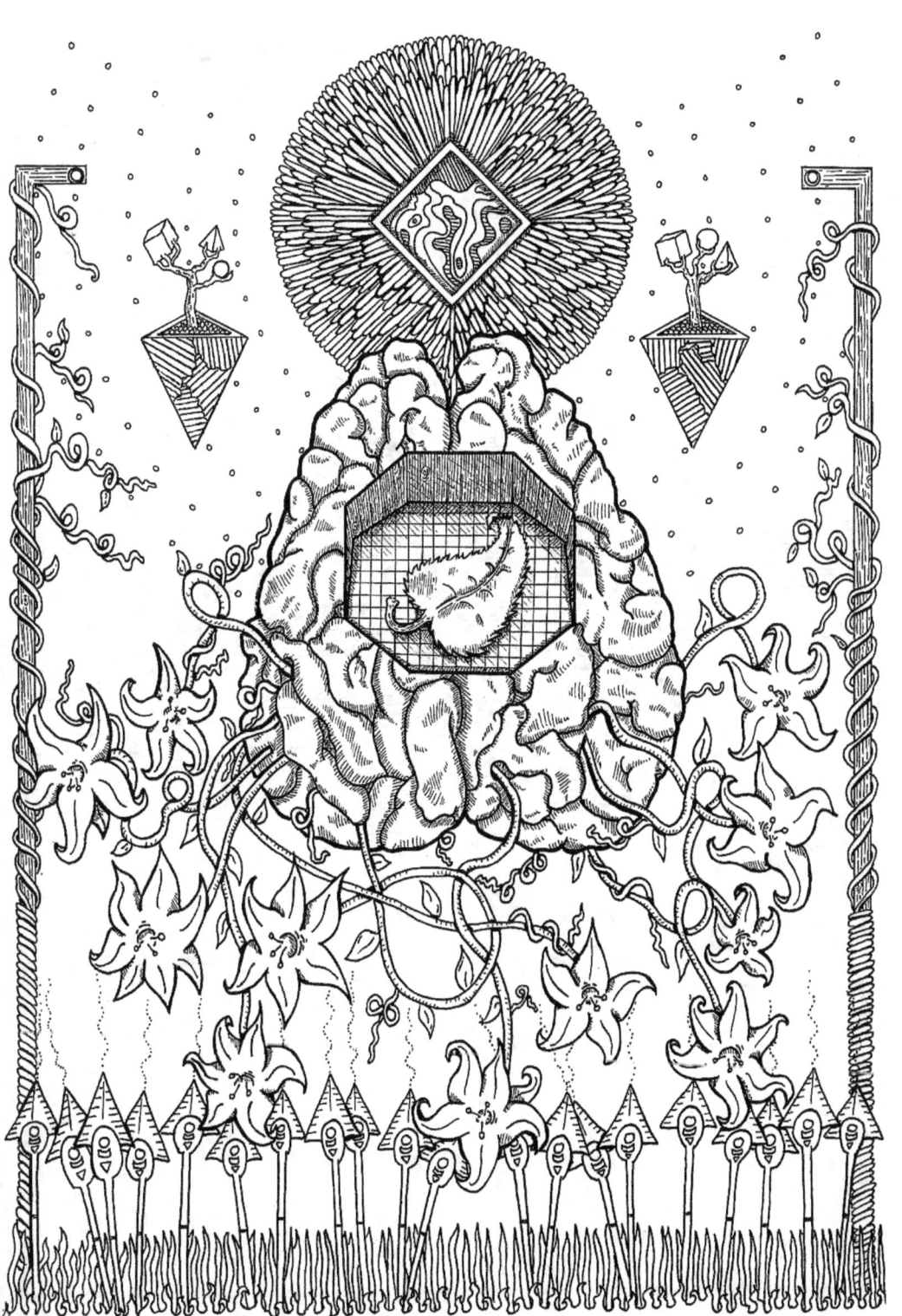

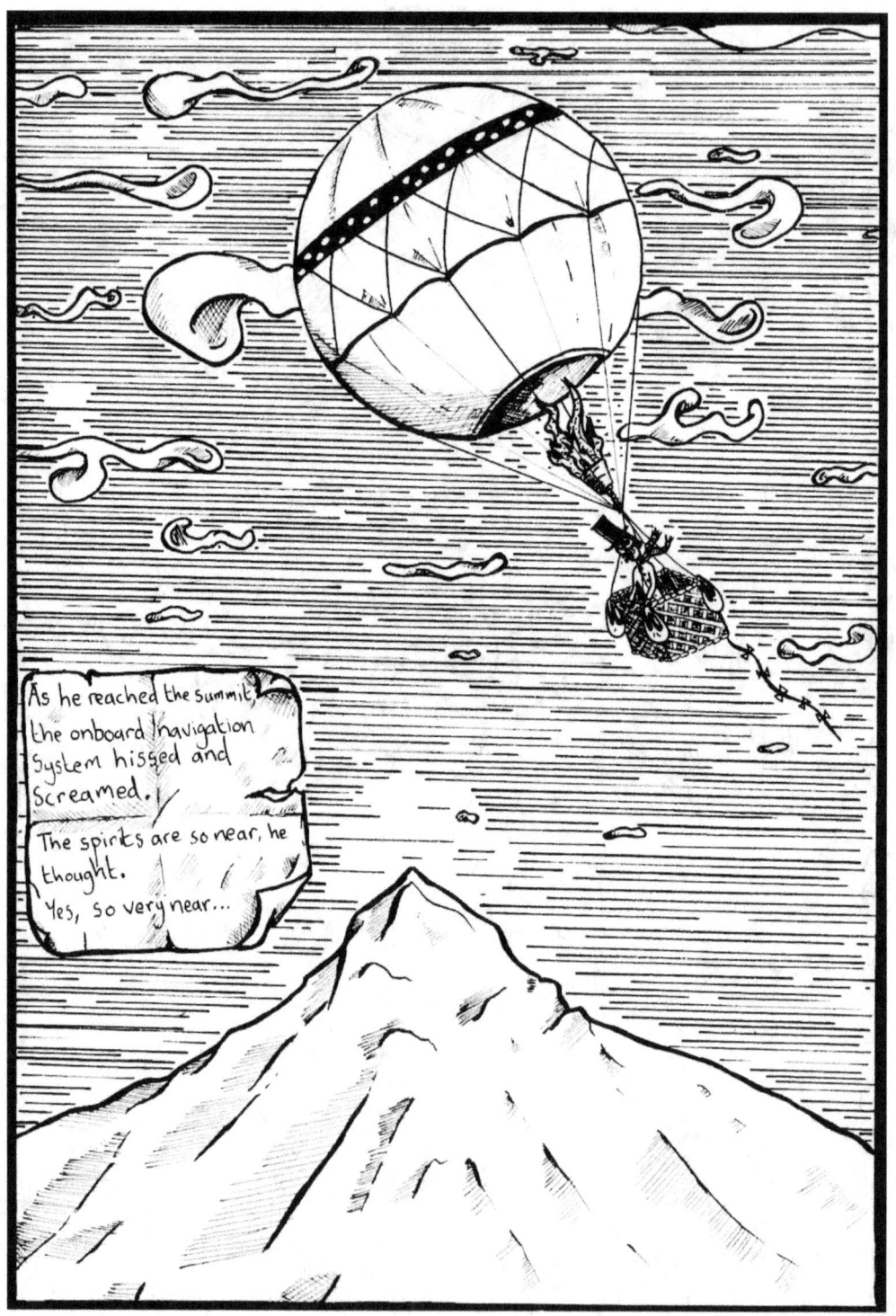

As he reached the summit, the onboard navigation system hissed and screamed.

The spirits are so near, he thought.

Yes, so very near...

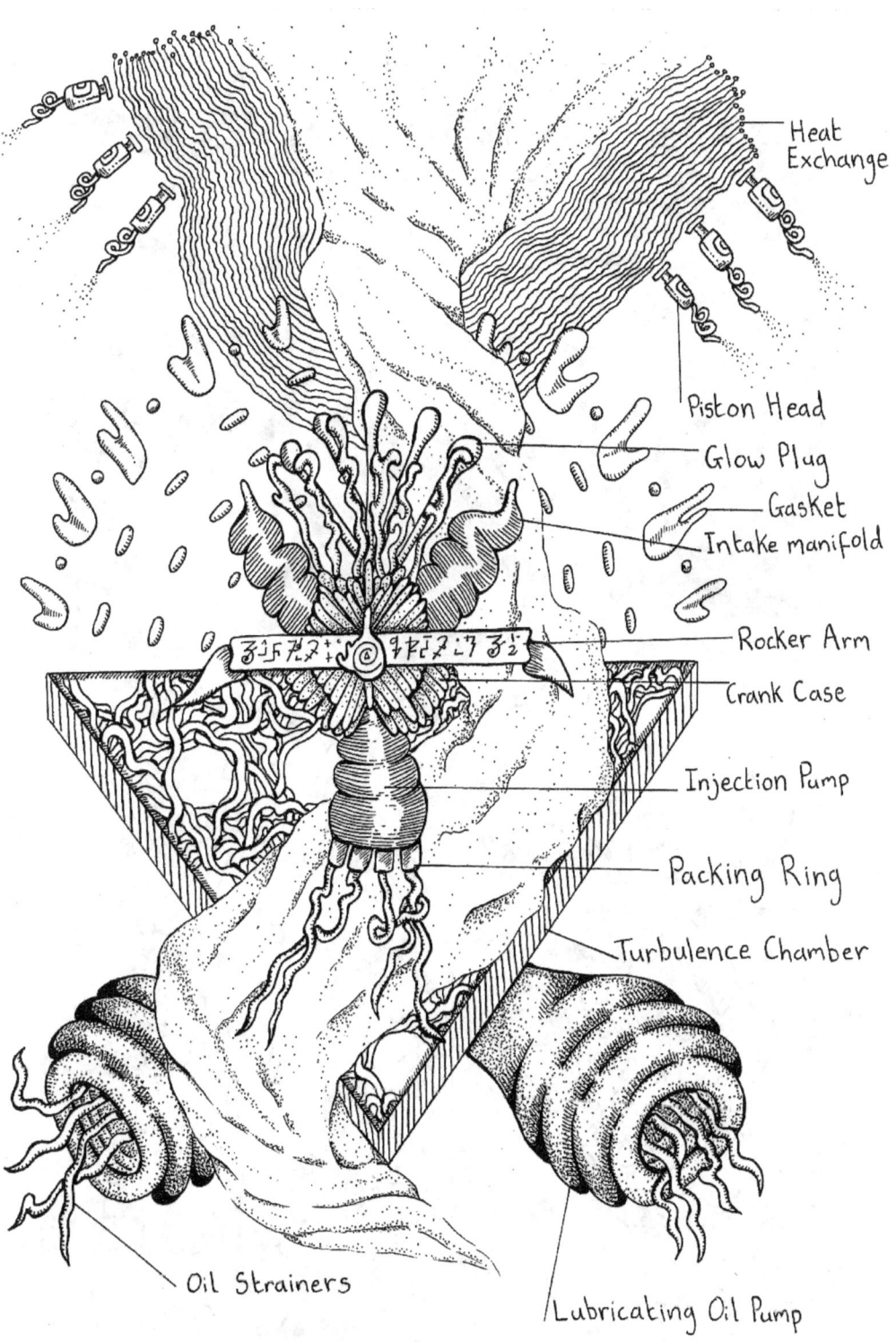

Heat Exchange

Piston Head

Glow Plug

Gasket

Intake manifold

Rocker Arm

Crank Case

Injection Pump

Packing Ring

Turbulence Chamber

Oil Strainers

Lubricating Oil Pump

Galactic Traveller 2xC9 Combustion Engine.

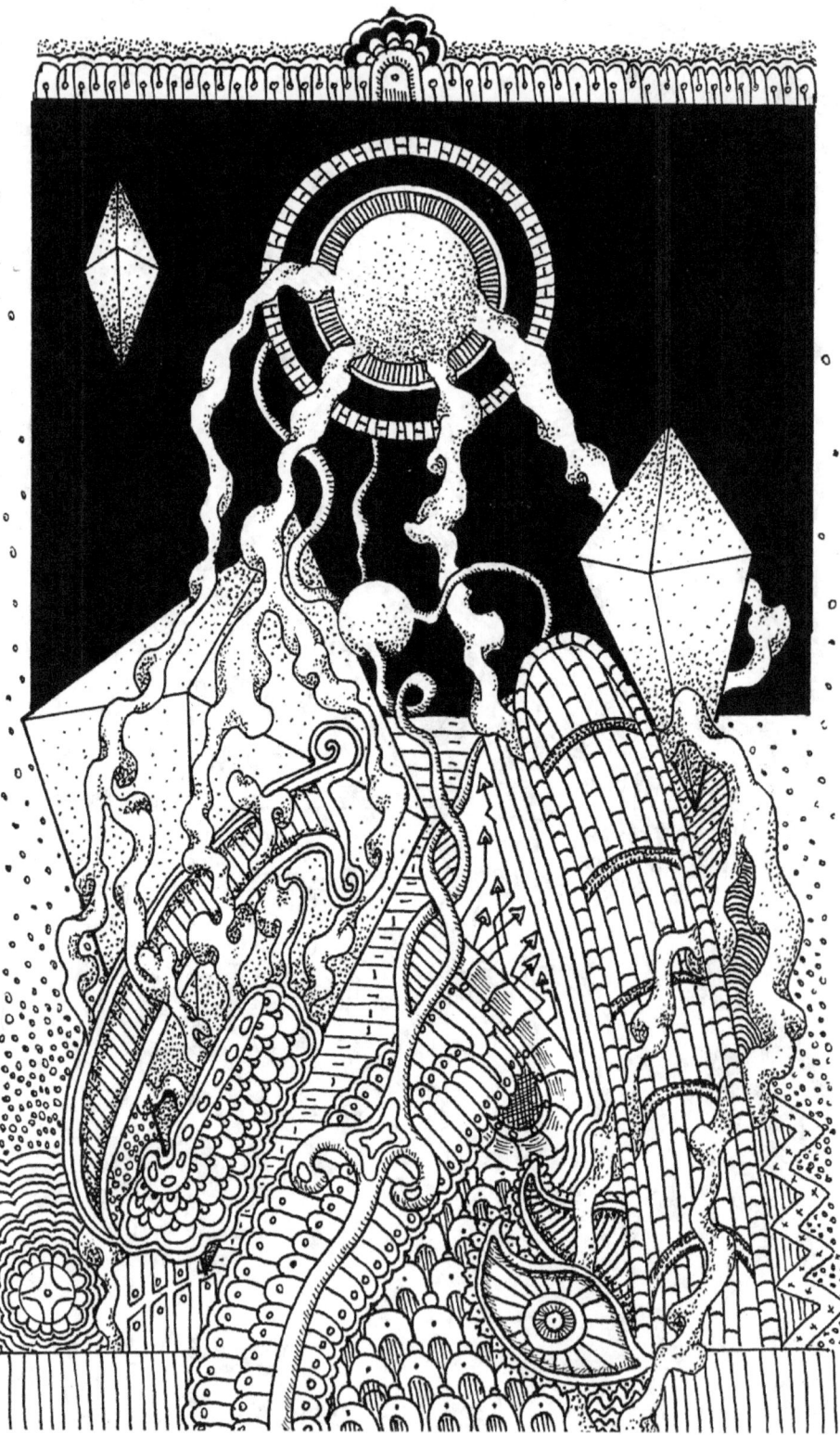

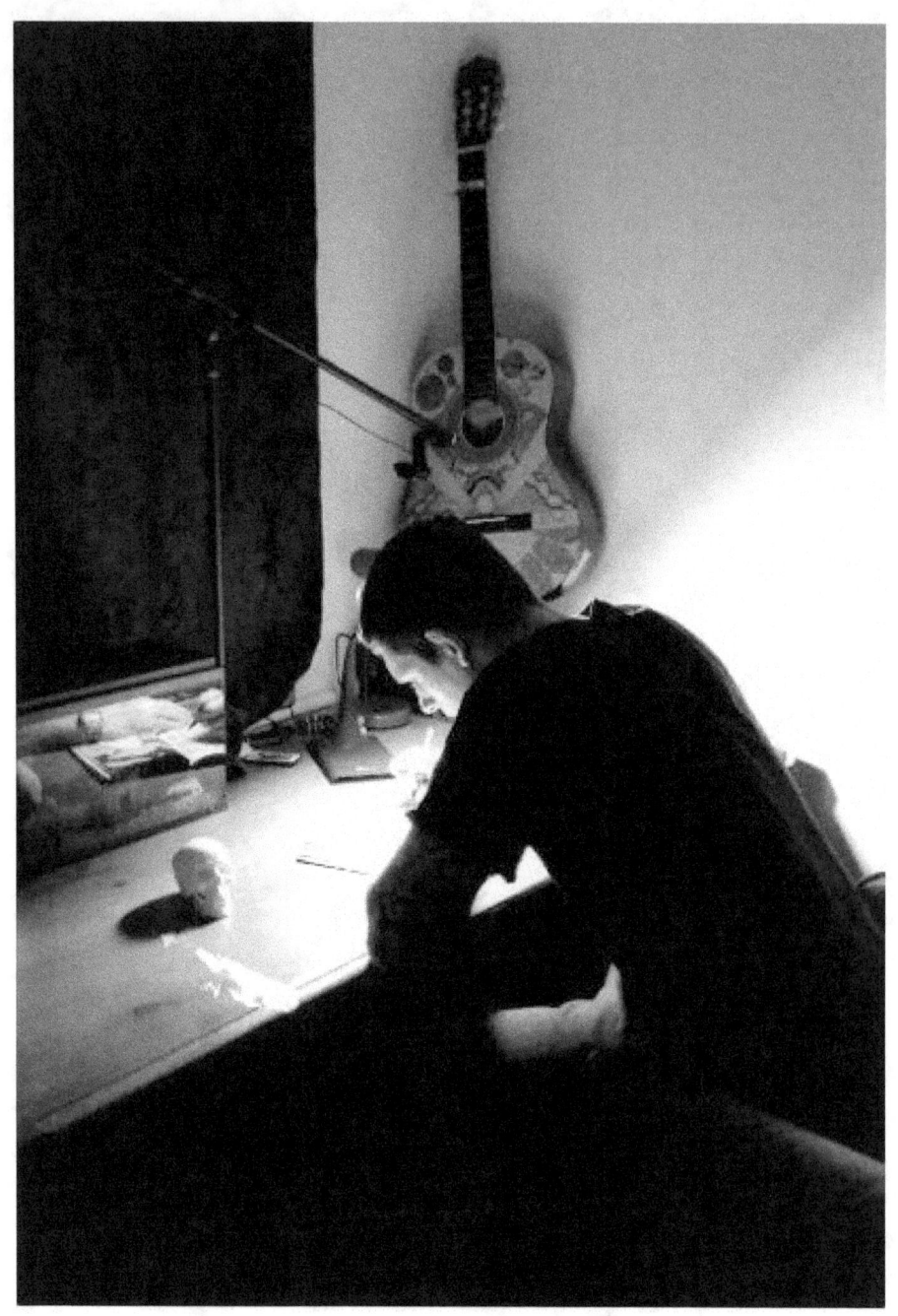

More to come...

If you enjoyed my book, then please review it on Amazon.

Thankyou

www.ingramcontent.com/pod-product-compliance
Lightning Source LLC
Chambersburg PA
CBHW072028190526
45166CB00015B/898